When a Customer Wins, Nobody Loses!

A Winning Formula for Building Lasting Customer Relationships

Gerry Brown

Text copyright @ February 2018

Gerry Brown

All Rights Reserved by

Gerry Brown

Published by Satin Publishing

ISBN-13: 978-1985150133
ISBN-10: 1985150131

Author Biography:

Gerry Brown aka The Customer Lifeguard, is on a mission to save the world from bad customer service. He helps businesses save customers at risk of defecting and breathes life into their customer service operations and customer experience strategy.

Gerry provides straight talking, no-nonsense advice and practical solutions for customer experience adoption and has provided organizational leadership on people development, business transformation, customer engagement and technology enablement for some of the largest companies in the UK, Canada, and EMEA. These include Autoglass, The Royal Albert Hall, O2, Screwfix, Sage, BSkyB, Bell Canada and TELUS

Gerry is a Member of the Professional Speaking Association (PSA), the Global Speakers Federation (GSF), the Customer Experience Professionals Association and a Certified Customer Experience Professional (CCXP).

Acknowledgement:

As a frustrated and often vocal customer myself, this book really has come from the heart and accurately mirrors my own feelings, opinions and attitudes towards the customer experience. But knowing that I wasn't alone, I've also benefitted from the collective wisdom of many friends and colleagues who, over the years, have inspired, supported and encouraged me in equal measure.

These include; Dave Carroll, Erwin Vinall, Jonty Pearce, Neil Davey, Sylvia Baldock, Michael Dodd, Mike Daglan, Bob Thompson, Bryan Barrow, Alan Stephens, Ken Hitchen, Ian Cavanagh, Gustavo Marin, John Busby, David Ashworth, Keith Wilkinson, Alan Barr, Lior Arussy, Steve Hyland and a host of other people who I haven't met in person, but whose emotional customer stories and positive actions have provided the impetus and themes that run throughout the book. Also, the companies that do get the ethos, and as a result have celebrated winning for their customers for many years, including all the deserved plaudits and success that goes with that. Not as long a list as we'd like, but includes; John Lewis Partnership, Metro Bank, First Direct, LL Bean, South West Airlines, Ace Hardware, Four Seasons Hotels, Ritz Carlton Hotels, Zappos, Screwfix, Homeserve and Autoglass.

And in a strange way, I have to thank all of the companies who have provided me with such appalling service so that I had no choice but to call them out. Perhaps some will actually take notice!

And a special thanks to Nicky Fitzmaurice at Satin Publishing for making sense out of the often jumbled contents of a clearly troubled mind and bringing them to life in a coherent manner!

Dedication:

To my long suffering and much loved and appreciated wife Maie Richards, who has listened patiently (mostly) with the appropriate empathy and encouragement, to my many rants about bad customer service and finally suggested in the strongest possible terms "to do something about it".

AUTHOR LINKS:

Twitter: *gerrybuk*

Facebook: *facebook.com/gerry.brown.73157*

LinkedIn: *www.linkedin.com/in/gerryhbrown*

Publisher Links:

SatinPaperbacks:

http://www.satinpublishing.co.uk
https://twitter.com/SatinPaperbacks
https://www.facebook.com/satinpublishing/

Email: nicky.fitzmaurice@satinpaperbacks.com

Contents:

Preface

During the Second World War, when Britain faced potential invasion and the loss of the war, the term 'Blitz Spirit' was coined; it is defined in the Oxford Dictionary as "Stoicism and determination in a difficult or dangerous situation, especially as displayed by a group of people." As privations through rationing continued for many years afterwards, this stoicism retreated into 'mustn't grumble' or 'mustn't complain', which continues to this day to be taken far too literally by much of the population. This attitude frequently results in unnecessary anger and frustration as businesses take advantage of this supine nature to underserve, overcharge and generally treat customers with disdain. They win, we lose!

In the wonderfully irreverent *Patronizing Bastards*, Quentin Lett's 2017 exposé on how the elites have betrayed Britain, he wastes no time in establishing one of his key themes. He nails the fundamental issue facing many of us in the losing camp; "Even the most docile beach donkey, if repeatedly kicked, will eventually refuse to cooperate. It will bare its long, yellow teeth and walk in the other direction, pulling its tethers out of the sand." And, as with any classic hero's journey, the downtrodden finally rise up and end up winning, whilst we all cheer them on.

Somebody Wins, Somebody Loses – Why?

I realize that the title of the book may be contentious. For many of us, growing up in a world where sport has played an important part in our lives, winning is seen as the ultimate goal. And losers are... well, losers. American Football fans may remember the Green Bay Packers' coach Vince Lombardi's famous quote, "Winning isn't everything, it's the only thing." Clearly that continues to be a familiar mantra in sport. Although the historians among you will also perhaps remember the American sports writer, Grantland Rice, who penned the poem 'Alumnus Football' that contained the line, "Not that you won or lost – But how you played the Game."

But in the business world, while companies want to be successful and be winners, it can't be achieved at all costs. It should be based on growing their businesses by helping their customers succeed – and win. Companies are beginning to realize that customer interactions can't be a zero sum game and a truly memorable, positive customer experience has to create value and be beneficial – for all the participants.

Helping customers win is a fundamental, founding principle for memorable customer experiences, even if your terminology and your definition of a win may be different. Winning in customer experience may be in making it incredibly easy for a customer to do business with you, or finding ways to surprise and delight them when they're least expecting it; these two objectives are not mutually exclusive. It could be in enabling and empowering your people to make decisions that are fair, equitable and clearly acceptable and valuable to the customer, or focusing on your customers' success rather than your own, although this is not an obvious goal for many businesses as yet. However, over the long term it's a philosophy and a strategy that will deliver the results that create a winning formula for both customers and the company. Furthermore, your employees will also feel a glow and the satisfaction that comes with doing the right thing.

In the final analysis, winning doesn't always mean getting everything you want. It means resolving issues or finding solutions where all parties gain more than they lose.

Winning is still a team effort

There is one analogy with sport that successful customer experience can share and that is creating a culture where the customer wins. It is also where customer experiences are intentional and consistently memorable achieved very much through a team effort and, like success in any field, it doesn't come easily. Those in a business who take on the task of creating better customer experiences must have resilience, tenacity and the ability to withstand criticism and doubt, especially from within their own organization. When done systematically, intelligently and inclusively, with a committed and organizationally supported cross-functional team, you can win customers' hearts and minds and enjoy the benefits that accrue. Be that as it may, patience, boldness and authenticity are also indispensable team members that are critical in winning over those who question the validity of what, for many, will be a new way of doing business.

It's often said that customer experience is everyone's responsibility within a business, however this may be an exaggeration if taken too literally (although I do believe that even the janitor can do their part). All the same, none of this happens by accident and, like any other worthy endeavour; a great customer experience starts with an innovative and creative design process that is a truly collaborative effort.

My experience has shown me that there are many willing participants, both inside and outside an organization and all employee and customer voices need to be heard, appreciated and actioned. Engaging and motivating the troops, willingly and visibly, is a noble and necessary element in creating great customer experiences. It's about people interacting emotionally and empathetically with people, and helping them as a natural consequence of being a fellow human. Much of it comes down to applying fundamental principles and ideals that we all know and most of us observe as we go through life, but seem to be forgotten or intentionally ignored in the Corporate world. These are basic human feelings, emotions, actions and responses that we exercise every day, without necessarily thinking about them or needing a manual to bring them to life.

Many organizations, especially those who seem to have mislaid (or never located) their moral compass, actively discourage their employees from displaying their human side and expect them to put their personal feelings, emotions and personality in a drawer marked "Not to be opened during business hours." While I'm not promoting anarchy or revolution (maybe a little of the latter), having an engagement strategy that features flexibility, agility and a sense of doing what is right, with some basic and sensible terms of engagement, will always win out over rigid autocratic rules and senseless, archaic policies.

As we'll see later in the book, the world of customer engagement, as with many things in business, has been changing quickly, unpredictably and irreversibly. The ever expanding influence of technology, especially social media and artificial intelligence (AI) on our lives; changing demographics, evolving work practices, political upheaval and just general global instability, have all come together to create a perfect storm that sweeps into our daily lives, and rains on our parade.

Consequently, we're seeing the rise of a new and very different type of consumer that won't take "Computer says no" for an answer. Consumers who demand actions that are measured in seconds and minutes, not hours or days, and who won't hesitate to share their discontent in less than sonorous tones via Twitter, Facebook and Instagram. Where conventional customer service technology such as telephone and even email seem archaic and headed for the scrap heap, (along with the people handling them if you believe some commentators), self-service, no service, chat bots named Gladys and AI are becoming the norm for many companies.

But it's not all doom and gloom. There is real hope for the future of customer engagement, irrespective of the methods, the media and the personnel, real or artificial, used by companies to interact with their customers. There are organizations that really get it and have clearly demonstrated their commitment to customers and colleagues that isn't just lip service. They apply some rational thinking, emotional connectivity, basic human decency, aligned with intelligent technology solutions that help customers win, make them happy and keep them coming back for more.

Inviting you to join this select group is the premise and the fundamental goal of the book. On this journey we'll look at resolving the most common challenges facing companies that are seeking to enhance customer engagement, increase retention, improve profitability, whilst reducing cost and employee attrition.

Before we go much further it's important to look at the different language being used to describe what goes on between customers and companies. You'll also undoubtedly see in this the book most of them stand up seeking attention. These include customer service, Customer Engagement, Customer Interactions, Customer Journeys and Customer Centricity. All of these are valid expressions that are used to describe different aspects of the customer-company relationships. While not necessarily interchangeable, they are inter-related and for our purposes we'll meet them under the umbrella of Customer Experience, or CX to its friends.

They'll be some examples of some well-known companies and ideas I've gleaned from my own local High Street that I feel can work in almost any business. Occasionally, when I introduce an example of great CX from an organization such as John Lewis, Zappos or First Direct, people often say, "But we're not..."I've also read blogs telling people to stop trying to be Amazon or Apple, but the bottom line is that irrespective of the size or type of business, there are lessons to be learnt everywhere, and all of these companies had to start somewhere.

I'm a great believer in the concept of marginal gains made famous by the Sky cycling team, even if the whiff of a drug related scandal appears to be making even bigger gains. Making small, incremental changes that can be implemented and evaluated quickly, but discarded if not effective, are key components of any transformation program and can be especially effective in a customer engagement scenario.

We'll look at how we got here, stars and dogs in the world of CX, potential roads to avoid in the future and finally an underlying framework and a clear path that will lead to a more democratized, engaged and trusting new consumer whose life expectancy is measured in years, not months. So, borrowing from the words of those well-meaning, but not entirely sincere or accurate, flight attendants, "Sit back, relax and enjoy the trip." When the customer wins, we all win.

Introduction

If you Googled 'customer experience' at almost any time in recent years, it's likely that you would have seen results in excess of 100 million hits. So where do you start? And as there is no shortage of books, articles, blogs and conferences on how to improve customer experience and customer service, why should you read this one? It's quite simple. It's based on real world situations and the concept of customers and companies both winning. It provides a strong foundational approach based on the simplicity of thought in the design of customer experience strategy. It avoids unnecessary complexity in its development and focuses on the value and strength of collective commitment and responsibility in its deployment and execution.

The approach is strongly aligned with the core principles that I'll introduce and refer to throughout the book, these ideas and concepts are adaptable for companies of all shapes and sizes. I have based this approach on my personal experiences and those of working with many different organizations, some of whom we'll meet in the book. We'll examine how the principles these companies use to develop enviable and sustainable reputations, create strong financial stability and establish high levels of employee engagement and customer advocacy, can translate into a customer experience that underpins and sustains their business success.

Let me introduce you to the Four Principles of Customer Experience, **Culture, Communication, Commitment and Community**. These are the foundations of a successful customer experience strategy and will be your travelling companions throughout the book and, I hope, for years to come during your customer adventures.

Customer experience strategy frequently calls on journey mapping as a key component to understanding the various touchpoints that a customer visits when interacting with a company. In any geographic adventure, visualizing your destination, having symbiotic travelling companions and planning the stopping points on the way are both necessary and enjoyable aspects of the trip.

This particular journey through the book will be landscaped with human emotions, signposted with empathy and common sense and then finished with a set of workable, adaptable ideas that can be deployed in a flexible and appropriate time-line that fits your overall business objectives. It's not meant to be *War and Peace*, more about peace and understanding for your customers and colleagues.

There are no complex charts, tricky quizzes, sexy graphics or other page-filling devices. Just common sense ideas, simply stated, easily started, quickly adopted and, I firmly believe, financially sensible in a number of ways that we will explore in more depth throughout the book. To further explain my approach, I'm borrowing a quote from *Alexandra*

K Trenfor. "The best teachers are those that show you where to look, but don't tell you what to see."

So we're not trying to visit every bay and cove along the rocky coastline of customer experience. This is a straight forward, no nonsense, outcome-based approach, that lays out the fundamental ingredients to successful customer engagement, but is often missing from the recipe.

- We'll start with a relatively short history lesson on where we are, how we got into this CX maze and how to get out. Then we'll look at why customers don't always see our point of view, or understand why we do what we do, or often, don't do.

- It will provide companies with guidance to understand who their customers are, what they expect and want, and don't want. How they can differentiate themselves from the competition with a strong customer experience culture and its relationships with their brand and the inherent promises it contains.

- The book will expand on the Four Principles and notwithstanding my desire to limit complexity, will identify in some depth how successful companies translate them into winning formulae for business success, and how the reader can learn from that success and apply the ideas in their own business.

- You'll understand how to gain the commitment and increase the contribution of all employees – the people side of the equation. In doing this, we'll help you create and sustain a corporate culture that pays more than lip service to customer centricity and builds long term, profitable customer relationships and strong employee performance and satisfaction.

- We'll review the technologies that will help you enable your customer experience strategy and support your most important stakeholders – customers and colleagues. But, we'll also examine why it's not the natural starting point for a customer experience revolution.

- We'll look at how you can effectively measure the results and align your customers' success with your own metrics, all based on mutual values and common goals.

- We'll complete the journey with a high level road map featuring actions you can take now that can inform and invigorate your own customer experience blueprint for customer experience action. We'll complement this with an associated set of actions you can do now that will get you started with a candid outside-in organizational review that will engage the wider community in the longer term effort, and still help bring your customer experience to life, and keep it running.

Nobody said that winning at business and delivering great customer experiences would be easy. But interacting with customers should be stimulating, uplifting, enjoyable and ultimately successful for both parties. After all, if they weren't there, what would you do? That really is a rhetorical question.

Irrespective of how the world turns, what technology evolves and who's on the end of a phone or a web chat, it's the principles, your values and how you incorporate them into your strategy that really matter. And that will ultimately result in a big win for your customers.

1. An Unlikely Hero

"We can beat them, just for one day. We can be heroes, just for one day" – David Bowie

On July 9, 2009, there was a seminal event in the world of customer service, and possibly in an even larger universe. This event had an unlikely geographic starting point and an even more unlikely but totally likable and sympathetic hero. Perhaps the only other surprise was that this "Black Swan" had such a long winter of discontent before finally showing us its plumage. But then again, the communication vehicle used to deliver what was to be a hammer blow to the already fading concept of the compliant customer was still a neophyte. However, it led to a sea change in the definition and influence of the new consumer and has become among other things, a weapon of mass brand and trust destruction.

Let me introduce the Canadian musician and folk hero Dave Carroll, whose YouTube video "United Breaks Guitars", had such an enormous impact when it hit the world of social media like a ton of guitars. For those unfamiliar with the story, Dave and his band had travelled from Halifax, Nova Scotia to Nebraska, via Chicago on United Airlines (UA). On the way, his Taylor guitar had been damaged by the UA baggage crew in Chicago. His attempts to get compensation from UA was met with disdain and disinterest by a number of UA employees and, after a saga lasting nine months, he decided that rather than getting mad, he'd get even. After writing a song about the experience and, with the help of some friends in Halifax, he put together a video that cost $150 and posted it on YouTube.

His objective was to get 1 million hits in a year, but had achieved that number within 4 days, along with a huge amount of media attention. The BBC reported the stock price of United Airlines dropped by $180 million that day, and while the share price may have recovered, that's not a headline that I'd want on my CEO CV.

Since then the video has truly gone viral and now has over 17 million hits and counting. It's not the first video to achieve a huge following, but the reason I believe that this was the tipping point in the ever changing customer service landscape, has been its longevity and continuing expanding influence. It's a story that plays and plays and is still shared by millions as if it's "new news".

No Lessons learnt here!

As I write this it is now almost 9 years later, March 2018. United Airlines customer service has hit new lows, and their latest YouTube video reached new viewing highs as they forcibly removed a customer who had been 'bumped' from a flight. Then BA had a complete computer meltdown, cancelled hundreds of flights and stranded thousands of customers for days. Then just when you thought it was safe to fly Ryanair again, they hit their customers with the cancellation of thousands of flights that they put down to "Messing up pilot holidays." The common themes running through all of these incidents were each company's inability to recognize the impact the events had, not to mention their massive failure to communicate or respond in a sensitive, empathetic and timely fashion.

Most people will understand that things don't always go right, but they also don't easily forgive or forget companies that fail to respond quickly, pro-actively and authentically when addressing the issues. Clearly, the original and subsequent United Airlines videos struck a chord with millions of disenfranchised and frustrated customers. This has led to many similar stories and resultant social and other media exposure about companies like UA, BA and Ryanair, who continue to ignore their customers' complaints and hope they'll just go away and leave them alone. More are doing just that by not flying with them and has led to a group being formed called *Anyone but BA* or ABBA. I guess their theme song might be "Take a chance on me" or perhaps "Ring Ring" reflecting the only thing that most customers hear when they call customer service!

I don't believe that these companies are just ignoring their customer's complaints – they are ignoring their customers completely or, amazingly, don't care about them. And it's not just me that thinks that. American business blogger and investor Tim Ferris asks a lot of people in his weekly podcasts "What would you put on a billboard?" Comedian Mike Birbiglia replied: "I'd put it in Times Square", where many businesses feature large and bold adverts and it would say, "None of these companies care about you." While that may be an extreme view, many businesses feel that investing in customer experience belongs in the 'too hard' or 'too expensive' pile. In case you think these are the musings of anti-capitalist, rabble-rouser, let me refer you to a well cited Rockefeller Corporation study that showed that 68% of customers leave a company because "They believe you don't care about them."

What else could explain the strange behaviour of United Airlines, BA and Ryanair, apart from the fact that they're airlines!

A Black Swan?

I earlier mentioned that the original UA story really was a *Black Swan*, or at least I believe it broadly meets the three criteria that Nassim Nicholas Taleb cites in his excellent book of the same name. For those of you who haven't paddled down the "Swanee" river, Taleb identifies three attributes that characterize a Black Swan event. First, it is an *outlier*, lying outside the realm of regular expectation (a non-celebrity, Dave Carroll, posting a video on YouTube, which was a far less regular occurrence in 2009). Second, it carries an extreme impact (17 million hits and a $180 million drop in share value). Third, despite its *outlier* status, people attempt to explain its occurrence after the fact, its retrospective predictability. (UA claimed that he was effectively just an unreasonable customer who hadn't followed proper procedures, otherwise they would have compensated him and it wouldn't have been necessary to post a video.)

Let them eat Cake! – But there'll be a charge for that

Now why did this collision of guitar and tarmac have such explosive qualities and what else has happened to change the attitudes and actions of customers? While I believe that this alone could have started the revolution, there is yet another key contributor to this perfect storm that resulted in more than just a broken G string, and focused even more attention on financial inequality and corporate misdeeds. This was the mad, bad economic tidal wave that rolled across the oceans of the world and is still washing up on the financial beaches of many countries and drowning their businesses.

Once again I turn to a renowned literary source for inspiration and validation. Ferdinand Mount, the author of the *"New Few Or A Very British Oligarchy"*, who argues very effectively that "Power and wealth in Britain, have slowly been consolidated in the hands of a small elite, while the rest of the country, (who recently have been brought to life via Theresa May's *Just About Managing* bunnies aka the JAMS) struggles financially and switches off politically." Nowhere was this more in evidence than the 2016 General Election in the UK, and it clearly had a similar impact on the US election in 2016. Although it's clear from both results, and the unexpected surge in Labour's popularity in the UK, that many have not only found the 'on' switch, but know how to work it.

While Mount doesn't explicitly make the connection between this central theme and a customer, it's not too much of a stretch to assume that the 'rest of the country' includes customers within their ranks. He recites a delightful and telling story about not being sorry about deserting Barclays Bank after having his account there for fifty years.

He goes on to say that "Barclays doesn't seem to be very sorry either, judging by the fact that I did not even receive a letter when I told them I was leaving. On the other hand the assistants in the branch were courtesy and sweetness itself. As always in my experience there was a **striking contrast** between the **solicitude** of the staff and the **indifference** of the top management."

Many people are quick to blame customer service employees when they have had a bad experience, but this is a soft, unfair and more often than not, wrong target for their ire. Increasing numbers of employees are recognizing the contrast that Mount references in his book, especially when they look at the huge discrepancies in pay with their leaders, and discover they are no longer willing to be embarrassed apologists for senseless, unexplainable rules and poorly designed and implemented customer service 'policies'.

The people at UA that Dave Carroll encountered were not inherently bad or intentionally rude. As he says in his book, *"I... was reminded again how my issue with the airline was about policies, not individuals."* But he was still probably the hundredth person that day to make a complaint or a claim, and the employees knew that their bosses would most likely berate them for even following through with it, let alone resolving it in the customer's favour, and so potentially affecting their executive bonus pot.

"We're mad as hell"

The expanding effects of the "Shareholder Spring" that first surfaced in 2013, also suggest that a return to the good old days of compliant and non-complaining customers is unlikely, although many companies continue to believe and hope that these 'milquetoasts' still exist in large numbers. Given that most shareholder revolts have been focusing on executive level remuneration, poor financial returns and benign, benevolent boards, there is a perceptible shift to the gathering storm of austerity-plagued, enraged, avenging customers, dispensing justice by taking their business elsewhere and trashing the company into the bargain.

Peter Finch's impassioned speech from the film *Network* (1976) and the 2017 London stage revival, "I'm mad as hell and not going to take it anymore", is primed and ready for full-on customer revival. What's interesting is that if you read the full version of the script, you'll see he's mad at pretty much the same thing that most people are going crazy about today.

A large portion of the world stopped trusting those in political power long ago as various global elections have continued to show us, even if it's still a "Hobson's Choice" in many countries. This was born out by the 2018 Edelman Global Trust Index (effectively a Net Promoter Score (NPS) for countries, institutions and businesses) that contained a plethora of telling and alarming statistics. The highlights included distrust in government as the default position, that 20 out of 28 countries (including the UK and US) are distrusters and that 42% of respondents said they didn't know what brands to trust.

This extends to almost anyone in a corporate leadership position. I'll spare you the lengthy list of those in the dock ranging from the banking, utility, telecoms and train company gangs, but you know who they are. People (customers) have been making their feelings known in ever increasing numbers and in more innovative ways, as social media platforms have made this task even easier. However, this isn't just a political argument; it's reflective of the frustration and anger that many people feel about so many aspects of society, including how they are treated as customers. While many have sought to politicize the various protest movements, the economic train wreck that has enveloped most countries has had broad ranging effects on most segments of society, except perhaps Senior Executives! The resultant letters to the editor, and affirmative action, has come from the *bien-pensant* of all political stripes.

As a regular 'Joe Bloggs' customer, I know that I'm as frustrated and certainly more angry and vocal about poor customer service than almost anyone else that I know. As I've noted in the Preface, I've spent much of my business life involved in various customer service endeavours, and it's the ongoing disconnect between what is being said, and actually being done by companies, that continues to amaze and disappoint me in equal measure.

Is it all just talk?

Every day I read articles, blogs, and receive invitations to attend webinars and conferences, (although my faith and interest in the latter is fading fast), where Senior Executives are continuing to <u>talk</u> about the importance of improving customer service and delivering a great customer experience, and that it's a key corporate strategic objective for 2018. The harsh reality is that you can substitute almost any year since 2010 for the last item.

However, despite this implied and often false sense of CEO care and urgency, my own experiences as a customer and that of a customer service practitioner, flies in the face of this newfound 'feeling of concern' for customers, and a recent survey from InMoment also supports this.

A significantly higher proportion of consumers in India (45%), Japan (38%) and Mexico (36%) think that companies 'value their business and will go the extra mile.' In Germany, the Netherlands (32%, each) and the UK (28%), finds more consumers believe that companies 'take their business for granted.' While in France (21%), Australia (13%), and Italy (12%) more consumers think that companies 'don't care about their business.' And this is backed up by an often cited Rockefeller Corporation study that said 68% of people stop doing business with a company because "They believe that you don't care about them."

Now these figures would be alarming even if everything was going along swimmingly economically. But, in today's world, shouldn't companies be going to extraordinary lengths to both win and retain customers and grow their businesses rather than the opposite?

When I first started thinking about putting my feelings into a book, I was going to title it 'The Death of Customer Service'. However, I soon realized that this wasn't really what was happening, and that some companies have very effectively and consistently resuscitated the patient.

Customers and their expectations are changing beyond all recognition, but many companies have been slow to recognize or react to this. Clearly they thought it would be much easier to address, and have neither devoted the time nor the financial investment required. But who said it would be easy? It takes a strong, committed and company-wide effort to slog through the treacle that is causing many businesses to become stuck in a morass of "We've always done it this way", or "We're as good as our competitors".

It'll be alright on the night

As I noted in the Preface and despite this gloomy introduction, I believe there is, as always, hope for the future. As with many cases in life, you can never go back and so perhaps while the customers as we know them have changed, there is emerging in their place a stronger, more well-informed, better connected (digitally) and less compliant consumer, stakeholder, client aka The New Consumer.

A major source of this new found strength is the power of social media and the Internet in general. This isn't going away anytime soon and tomorrow's New Consumer will have no truck with being forgotten in long phone queues, let down by poor websites, or misunderstood by disinterested, powerless customer service agents. Companies that fail to see this shift and continue as if nothing has changed, will themselves be lined up in the corporate obituary columns.

I believe that the New Consumer will join forces with the shareholder activists in a new, powerful and effective coalition that will convince companies, perhaps kicking and screaming, to work cooperatively with them for their mutual good. Those businesses that go willingly and recognize, cultivate and embrace these newbies, will survive and prosper. This may not be a formal coalition but, as with many movements, political or otherwise, they will gather momentum through shared values and interests, or simply as a marriage of convenience.

A dazzling and uncomfortably blinding spotlight will shine on those businesses that are making short-sighted, ill-informed decisions to cut costs, especially those associated with reduced investment in staff education, hiring and technology that actually end up decreasing the value and profitability of the company. (Many banks faced with finding money to pay huge fines for their previous misdeeds are making the most of the large deposits in this account.) These reactive decisions to wield the knife are based on these companies' perception of shareholders' financial prudence expectations, and perhaps ironically, are self-defeating insomuch as the opposite could actually deliver improved financial performance. In some cases, companies are deciding not to invest at all in the initiatives that could have a beneficial effect on customer service, based on the flawed theory that doing nothing and hoping that customers will 'get over it', is financially responsible and operationally valid. Not unsurprisingly, the potential cost of investments in improving customer experience pale in comparison to even moderate executive remuneration.

Once again, the fundamental issue at work here is the total loss of trust that is felt by customers, and that can be the death knell for any relationship. Rebuilding that trust will take time and for many businesses and industries this may take a total reorganization with a totally new and sustainable strategy. When the New Consumers look at companies that consistently get rave customer reviews, such as Zappos, John Lewis and Metro Bank, they'll make another valuable connection. They'll see that these companies, which actually invest more money to improve their quality of service, staff, technology and processes (rather than just spewing out the rhetoric and auditioning Z-list celebrities to promote their products), are not only making money, and yes, increasing their shareholder value, but they are also staying under the combative press radar and away from the toxic headlines that are deemed deadly for customer relations and employee morale.

2. The Gathering Storm –
   The Digital Natives are Getting Restless

"Those Apaches look dangerous, Tonto – I think we could be in trouble. What do you mean, 'we' Kemosabe?"

Over 200 years ago, a humorous book entitled *The Miseries of Human Life* was written by the Reverend James Beresford. It was a satirical and ironic tome that recorded and praised the causes of discomfort in early 19th century England, what we would now term as 'first world problems'. It was subtitled the *Groans of Samuel Sensitive and Timothy Testy*, and catalogued in excruciating detail the "Petty outrages, minor humiliations, and tiny discomforts that make up every day human existence." The Miseries were written as a series of discussions between Mr Samuel Sensitive and Mr Timothy Testy, in which they catalogue the daily "Injuries, insults, disappointments and treacheries" of everyday life. We now do this via *Facebook*.

A Nation of Moaners

In the early years of the new millennium, the descendants of the possibly mythical Messrs. Testy and Sensitive have turned groans into moans and made them an art form. The English are now known as a nation of moaners, according to recent research from the Ombudsman Service published in *The Times*. They calculated that there are now 52 million complaints a year made to social media, supplier complaint lines, ombudsman services and small claims court. However, the research also noted that another 66 million problems had not led to complaints, with many put off by the effort involved. But if encouraging affirmative action had been the intention of the good Reverend, would that have satiated the myriad moaning needs of the early nineteenth century population? Later reviews of *The Miseries* suggested that the book, rather than being an early example of a self-help guide, became the opposite. Partly, it was said at the time, "Because grumbling is to the grumbler so sweet a luxury, and misery to the miserable, so dear a happiness, actually finding relief was totally inconsequential and in fact ruined the sport."

However, things are changing in this brave new world of "Taking back our country", "Standing up for the little guy", "For the many, not the few" and other noteworthy, but possibly unachievable visions of Camelot; a world where millions have voted for a navigational change into what is clearly unchartered waters and undiscovered territory, without too much understanding of the tsunami that awaits them. But where is the righteous and demonstrable anger that should be directed at many of the so called 'Senior Executives' running businesses into administration, then lining their own pockets while constantly and surreptitiously putting their hand in ours? Especially as they are doing this by providing a truly appalling service and dealing from the bottom of the deck of broken service promises. Don't take my word for it though, think about your own anecdotal evidence as customers and the stats from regular surveys from the likes of Which? Magazine and the Institute for Customer Service (ICS). As customer service in the UK continues to slide precipitously over the cliff of disinterest into the gaping chasm of incompetence, I wonder what it will take to reverse the charge of the lemmings?

A customer service revolution - storming the boardrooms?

Where do revolutions start? Do they develop from the thinnest sliver of injustice in one person's mind such as Dave Carroll and UA? Or are they fermented in the huge and constantly boiling vat of prejudice, hatred and oppression that seems to blight our world even more now than it ever did. No one generation has the monopoly on horrific deeds committed under the banner of revolutionary fervour, and this is now continually whipped up into an ongoing multi-media storm that floods our homes and our consciousness with unrelenting regularity. The images created in our minds, both real and supposed, are so much more thought provoking and anger-generating by virtue of their vibrant colour and texture that modern media brings to our vision. The storm clouds are gathering and that rumble that you hear is coming from the Millennials, Gen X, Y and Z, the so-called digital natives who will be a very different audience; much less compliant, less patient and far more filled with revolutionary zeal.

When we look back at late 18th century France or early 20th Russia, we can be easily persuaded (or perhaps fooled), that those revolutions were the natural result of citizens feeling angered by a depraved, cruel and out of touch monarchy. There's no question that there is substantial historical evidence to back that up, but what was it that pushed the first French patriot to tire of cake and promises and utter those mortal words that incited the rest of the population "To the Bastille"?

Let down most by the companies we really count on

Will organizational impotency, corporate cowardice, executive incompetence be the trigger for the next populist movement, if it hasn't already? Every hour of every day, of every year we are overcharged, under-served and generally treated with disdain by many of the companies we do business with. This isn't a sensationalist war cry or gross exaggeration. Think about the level of 'service' that we get from the companies that we all daily rely on to manage our lives. The banks, telecoms companies, utility providers, insurance companies, airlines and the worst of the worst; the train companies.

Perhaps another way to look at this would be to rate the depths of deception that these companies have reached by aligning them with the fines they have paid for swindling, misleading, under serving and generally ripping us off with impunity. I say impunity because the fines don't seem to have an effect, especially as they seldom affect real change or make a dent in the company's profits.

But it's not just me that thinks this. A recent letter in the Sunday Times with the headline *"Business must rediscover its moral compass"* put it neatly and articulately in perspective. The writer was responding to the mixed messages that were emanating from the 2016 UK General Election and the apparent socialist agenda that was developing, and summarized it as follows:

"One only has to look at a few media stories to understand how I, and many others, view big business: alleged fraud (Barclays); cheating its business customers (RBS); greedy exploitation (Philip Green); tax avoidance (Google, Starbucks, Amazon, Facebook) and poor employment standards (JD Sports, Uber)."

With the customer service bar in many businesses set lower than savings' interest rates, it's really a race to the bottom to be the worst performers. In Which? Magazine's latest poll of 100 UK brands, all of the brands placed 90th or lower are utilities, mobile phones companies, landlines, broadband or TV services and the train companies don't even make the list! Many of these have been there consistently over the years and, beyond surveys, regularly make the headlines and helplines for truly appalling customer service.

So how do we affect change? Many industries, especially financial services and utilities, cling to the out-dated idea of self-regulation as the shield that can hold off the angry hordes. Taken from the theme of "Dance as if no one's watching", and translate to "Serve as if no one's listening". In the case of Supervisor or Managers in observational mode, this doesn't seem to be working. Even the mostly impotent and feeble regulatory bodies such as Ofcom, Ofgem and Ofwat (known as the Tut-Tut Brigade in Quentin Letts' excellent book *Patronizing Bastards*), do occasionally slow down the runaway train of corporate arrogance and irresponsibility, such as the recent and long overdue BT and Open Reach decision. How likely is that to bring about the transformational change necessary for the public good? While companies such as BT, EE and their ilk make major contributions to worsening many people's economic struggles, these issues are relatively mild when compared to more serious crises in many parts of the world. That doesn't mean however, that we shouldn't seek to dramatically change how many of our 'leading' businesses treat us.

It's in your hands, or feet

But wait, there seems to be a solution, and the good news is that people don't have to wait for an official referendum or a badly timed election. The opportunity is in their hands, their feet or their dialling and clicking fingers every moment. At any time they can make what seems like a small gesture by switching bank or energy provider, but as we've seen, and has regularly been reported by Which? and other commentators, we're still reluctant to do this in the numbers required to truly get the captains of industry to abandon their Mediterranean cruise ships and face the harsh economic reality.

Getting the trains to work as expected is certainly going to take a little longer. This group of operational incompetents, ably aided and abetted by their lame, pandering, in-house apologists The Rail Delivery Group, will resist any challenge to the corporate oligarchy and near monopoly to their very last overpriced ticket and late-running, over-crowded train. There doesn't appear to be any help coming from the government in the form of the current transport minister Chris Grayling either, whose main role seems to be bailing out 'ailing' train franchises rather than addressing the inexplicable and confusing ticketing policies, ongoing strikes and general mismanagement. But now the UK government has even bigger problems of their own to address, so don't hold your breath for that one.

In case you're wondering, I'm not really a disciple of Lenin, Che Guevara or Fidel Castro. I'm probably more George Washington or FDR in attitude and desire, if not in capability or reputation. I really would like to see businesses succeed and prosper for the right reasons, by providing valuable products and services, timely and truly helpful effortless customer engagement, while treating employees with respect, equanimity and courtesy. Alas many arrogant, insincere and self-serving companies only pay lip service to that objective with slick marketing campaigns and executive bafflegab. Fortunately there are some examples of great corporate leadership and caring businesses to learn from, and as we continue on our journey with the Four Principles as our guide, we'll examine these in more detail.

But we still have to deal with those pesky customers.

3. So what exactly is a Customer? And where did it all go wrong?

"Maybe the most that you can expect from a relationship that goes bad is to come out of it with a few good songs" – Marianne Faithful

It will definitely help when we know what "The Customer" looks like, or looked like if we've lost track of that. However, that may be a step too far for many companies as they seem totally incapable of knowing a customer, or truly interpreting their needs when they see one.

For many businesses their definition of a 'Customer', or in fact their very use of the word seems to be uncomfortable. Here are two definitions:

1) A person or organization that buys goods or services from a store or other business.

2) A person or thing of a specified kind that one has to deal with: 'a tough customer'.

The origin of the term was taken from the 14th century 'customs official', later 'buyer' (early 15th century, from the Anglo-French, *Custumer)*. A more generalized meaning "A person with whom one has dealings" emerged in the 1540s; that of "A person to deal with". In Shakespeare, the word also can mean 'prostitute'." Hmm!

Now clearly, we could turn this into a semantic argument and I certainly do want to explore different types of customers throughout the book, but let's start with the first definition.

At first glance we could argue that this most basic of descriptions still applies today and very simplistically answers the 'what is' question. But dig a little deeper and start asking some 'how', 'what', 'where' and 'why' questions, then the picture changes dramatically.

I recognize that customers still walk into shops and carry on a face-to-face conversation with an employee. They are expecting (or hoping) that the interaction will be positive, filled with useful information and delivered with a smile. It is, however, very likely that many customers will have already done significant research on-line, that they will have checked out community sites, or read customer reviews before setting foot in the store. It is then, at the first sight of a negative experience, based on price, product capability, employee knowledge or other red flags, they will reach for their smart phone and show the employee what they can get somewhere else.

As far as today's customers are concerned, the old rules no longer apply. Whenever they have a problem with a product or service, the chances of them picking up the phone and calling customer service, especially when it costs them money, and inevitably end up talking to somebody who appears out of touch with their situation and furthermore is powerless to offer anything more than platitudes, is increasingly unlikely. But we still do it.

The Power behind the Phone -They've got you by the Calls!

"If you've got them by the balls, their hearts and minds will follow." - Theodore Roosevelt

The man sat transfixed in terrified anticipation. His mouth was dry, but sweat poured from his brow and slowly dripped down onto the desk in front of him. His knees shook and his hands trembled and moved slowly, but inexorably to the very instrument that could be the source of further pain but may also lead the way to a form of salvation. He knew that he was going to be going down a dark and frightening road from which there may be no way out and that he had never been down before. He knew of friends and relatives that had preceded him on this difficult journey and could only imagine the suffering, pain and anguish that they had gone through. But he knew that he could go on no longer, time was running out and a decision had to be made.

He was, of course, going to call his mobile phone company's contact centre to renew his contract and upgrade his phone, and while perhaps this isn't everyone's experience, I'm sure that you've all felt the same trepidation when you have to make that call to any customer service organization. Will I get trapped in a maze of deadly automated systems when no real person is there? Will the same personal identification questions be asked repeatedly, even if I've given all of this when I first called and I have a password to shortcut this process? Will the agent say "Obviously" one hundred times during the course of the call, even though nothing is obvious? All the while knowing that whatever you ask of them they won't have the right information available to them. The information that is right for <u>you</u>.

Now while I'm using a mobile phone company as an example, I don't want you to think that I'm just picking on them because most of them are continually at the bottom of almost any CX league table! Because almost any call or interaction with a bank, a utility company of any company that you care to name can be the source of extreme frustration and take a huge chunk out of many people's busy day. Why should this be? Why should we be the ones who are afraid? After all we know what we want, don't we?

What do customers really want?

Many businesses believe that they know their customers' needs and wants better than their customers do.

"If I had asked people what they wanted, they would have said faster horses."

This quote, attributed to Henry Ford, but probably apocryphal, has been doing the rounds for some time. The underlying message however, and a challenge still faced by businesses worldwide today, is whether or not customers really know what they want from a company. This was brought into even sharper focus when Steve Jobs said,

"It's really hard to design products by focus groups. A lot of times, people don't know what they want until you show it to them."

This attitude may be excused when it comes to product development, but needs a serious overhaul when it relates to how customers want and expect to be treated.

In 2018, it's not only trying to figure out what customers want, but how and where they want to consume the products and services businesses are trying to sell them. In Henry Ford's day and for most of the 20th century and early 21st, if you wanted a car, you simply went to a car dealer. While this is still probably the preferred way of doing things, buying a car on-line and taking a 'virtual' test drive is becoming more common. This is backed up by recent stats from Auto Trader showing that forecourt visits have dropped by over 50 % in the last five years. And their survey also showed that for many people the fear of a contact centre interaction is probably only outstripped by that of encountering a car salesperson!

Researching a car purchase is just one example of the changing way in which we interact with businesses and is just one step in the circuitous and definitely non-linear, customer journey that has many twists and turns. Figuring out the 'how', 'what', 'where', 'when' and 'why' of your customer interactions are key elements within the increasingly important topic of Customer Experience that seems to be high on most Senior Executive's agenda. To deliver the experience a customer wants and expects, when they want it and how they want to consume it, you need to start with all of the data that could possibly be related to and/or impact their journey across your enterprise. This includes the related components, (partners, big data, structured and unstructured information), and you need to be able to have all of this available constantly, consistently and in real time. So this means your employees and/or self-service solutions need to access any system, anywhere quickly and with very low overhead. Now that's the perfect world and while you shouldn't give up on reaching that Utopian plateau, it will undoubtedly require some operational changes.

We'll take a deeper dive into the technology side of that later in the book. But in the meantime, there are customers to be attained, maintained and retained, who have ever changing expectations of their relationships with you. Knowing their preferences, their moods, what makes them tick, and the reality that it's never the same experience twice, are major clues to meeting those expectations each and every time.

What's the big deal about big data?

With all the focus on the importance of big data, (and I'm not disputing this), we also need to start thinking about all the ways that companies can meet changing expectations in customer interactions without investing a small fortune and taking months or years to do it. A major step is enabling businesses to maximise the value they can derive from existing data, real time analytics, frequent feedback and research, to intelligently interact with their customers and develop a data and insight strategy that has four main elements.

i. Firstly, you need to figure out the specific challenges facing your business that more effective use of data can address. Start by identifying some **carefully selected**, but relatively **simple and available** pieces of information that could help you target and convert more effectively. This could be last order date, order value, feedback score or other key data that you should have already or can find in other existing systems.

ii. Then, blending that with what you already know about your customers and prospects. The insight that you gain needs to be **actionable** and **contextual,** to help you make timely offers, or address issues that can provide **immediate, valuable** and **recognizable** benefits to the customer. This could be based on their anniversary as a customer, data on all their purchases and previous problem flashpoints or issues.

iii. Next, the offers need to be **relevant** and **closely matched** to the customer's profile and growth potential while still being readily visible and accessible to customer sales/service staff or when a customer self-serves. Ideally something that aligns with their demographic and avoids those things that don't match. An example of this is an email I received about opening a student bank account from a financial services company that I already did business with and who would have seen that my date of birth used Roman numerals.

iv.   Finally, the offers must be **personalized,** using **behavioural** insights and **content rich** so that the recipient can see that you've used their information intelligently and that you understand their needs, wants and preferences. This alone can win over many cynical customers who are frustrated with getting "Dear >name<" emails, or similarly bad examples of companies that can't be bothered to even get the basics right.

There are many real or perceived challenges about Big Data, and data in general, especially with GDPR looming on the European horizon, not the least of which is agreeing on what 'data' really is and how to gather and use it, effectively and appropriately. Here is where I believe that size doesn't matter, but that the *quality, insight* and the *immediate actionability* gained is far more important and can have a profound and sustainable effect on both customers and the company.

I had a chance to test this out this out on a recent trip to Canada. I met with a team from a growing software company that I had worked with previously, and who were looking to improve their performance in terms of both existing customers and new business. However, they didn't have a huge amount to invest in gathering and collating a lot of 'new' or Big Data. We looked at what they already knew about their customers and prospects and decided that it was worth seeing if adding some carefully selected, but relatively small and actionable pieces of information, would help them target and convert more effectively.

Once they'd decided on what they thought would be valuable, they added a section on the login page where prospects could download information. It provided a brief intro about the mutual benefits of fulfilling the request and then asked customers to take a few moments to update their data and to add some new information. They promised not to sell the list and also asked if they wanted to opt out, so effectively not participating in the exercise. Most people agreed and provided more good info, which was no real surprise as we all know that Canadians are very nice people and not at all boring! (I can say that, I do have the passport.)

One of the critical, but simple elements to success was asking people to input some additional, personalized information on their business and buying habits. As a result, their lead conversion rate improved by 22% and their sales to existing customers jumped by 6%. Both numbers translated into some reasonably serious revenue, while also increasing the feel good factor with their customers. And the really great part was that other than agreeing on the information needed and designing a very easy to follow landing page, their costs were minimal and it was all done with very little human intervention. They were using Salesforce, so it was really easy to have the updated details find their way into the contact record and then to run a short report that identified who had applied the update. It was simple, measurable, repeatable and profitable and definitely a winning combination for all parties.

OK so we've got this data, but where is it when we need it?

Even if a company has an unlimited budget and/or IT resources that can crack the Big Data nut, the challenge that many businesses face is that information and customer data reside in different places and in different forms - usually in the often maligned, ageing legacy systems that companies are finding expensive to replace or modify.

Why it's important to address this ever increasing fusion of critical customer data can be summed up in one word - **Immediacy**. Customers reach out from many places, in different ways and usually without much warning. What they want more than anything is recognition of who they are; what their issues are; and how quickly and smoothly they will be addressed.

The key is to have a unified view of every customer interaction within the organisation, whether it's with marketing, service or sales, and whether it's taken place via email, web, phone, social media, chat, messaging or posts in the community forum. Many businesses see those interactions as separate and distinct transactions, and that the utopia referred to as a 360° or single customer view is unattainable. It's not, and its validity is non-negotiable. In order to address the immediacy and service levels that customers want and expect, it's vital to bring all those individual transactions together to show the customer's interaction history with the business. This enables colleagues and self-service operations to better understand the customer, to provide a better answer in a shorter time, and a timely, more personalised service experience for the customer every time.

The solutions that zero in on this most effectively are usually cloud based interaction platforms that can provide immediate, updated and visual access to customer history, regardless of channel, and are integrated within a single window that can access the legacy big boys when necessary. This makes them easier to use and deliver faster response times without having to switch applications and/or significantly adding to the existing IT infrastructure.

The provenance of these solutions varies from CRM to contact centre and other customer service focused applications, but are generally aimed at maintaining, consolidating and displaying customer contact data across channels and locations. They usually feature more open Application Programming Interfaces (API) that can make system integration easier, quicker and much less expensive. Companies will find that, even if they are committed financially and contractually to their older legacy systems, they can still use the cloud to push and pull data to and from the right places, thereby increasing their ability to provide an updated, accurate view of the customer and deliver a greater customer experience.

Cloud technologies also have their share of doubting Thomas's, usually in IT, and there is no single journey map to cloud adoption, but rather a wide variety of on-ramps and paths. Organizations have different starting points, goals and available resources. Consequently, in the interests of corporate harmony, an amalgamation of traditional IT solutions and methodologies that provide an evolution, rather than a revolution, is the way that many companies are building cost effective, technological solutions aimed at enhancing customer engagement, regardless of the channel. This is the Omni-channel world that can provide a seamless journey for the customer and a consistent and inclusive view of customer history for the employee.

Many cloud solutions offer low cost, or no cost, trial periods that allow organizations to test the applications as part of a Proof of Value (POV) program in a real world or test environment, before deciding to proceed. As a subscription model, companies can also manage their investment carefully, and users can be brought on as required with flexibility in both data and capability, and with a minimum of IT involvement and additional, expensive on-site hardware.

Many organizations are now looking at implementing cloud based model offices and innovation hubs as a way to conduct discovery exercises and fast track strategic, procedural and operational developments. These POV environments enable them to trial these concepts in 'what if' scenarios that can mirror customer behaviour, colleague actions and determine acceptance of the proposed changes or any obstacles to their introduction.

Even if an organization needs to go to tender, they can go with a much clearer idea of requirements, and knowledge of the "Art of the possible" that can significantly reduce procurement time frames and costs. This is probably the single best investment that you can make in technology to enable your customer experience strategy. But it's not the only one and we'll see more in chapter 8.

It's becoming evident from increasing company adoption that businesses reaching for the cloud will find that these solutions can make life easier, quicker and satisfying for customers, smoother and less time consuming for colleagues and more cost effective for the business, and that's got to be better than having your head in the sand, which is where many companies find themselves buried.

4. This Customer Experience stuff can't be that hard, can it?

*"Don't we just hand out hats, T-shirts and mugs that say the "Customer is number 1" – **Ex** CEO*

When the **Harvard Business Review** article entitled *"Stop Trying to Delight Your Customers"* first appeared in July 2010, the axles on the bandwagon of the newest shiny metric, the Customer Effort Score (CES), noticeably sagged under the strain of the new disciples jumping on-board. In a nutshell, the article opined that delighting your customers was a waste of time and money, when all they really wanted was for you to make it easier to do business with them, and to reduce their effort, irrespective of how and when they contacted you.

Since then, the authors have published a very readable book called *The Effortless Experience* and an increasing number of articles have been published with a similar theme. The comments and/or attention grabbing blog posts include:

"Why focusing on delighting your customers is a stupid strategy."
"Don't bother with WOW."
"Just make it easy for your customers."

I should state right here that I'm in total agreement with the overall concept of making life easier, and particularly with one of the conclusions in the book that I believe to be the central plank in the argument:

"It turns out that the overwhelming majority of customers aren't looking to have their expectations exceeded. They simply want their service experience to be easy."

To me, the crucial words are the 'service experience' and by extension, what I take to be a *'customer service experience'*. However, as already stated, it's so much more than just an interaction with an employee in a contact centre, in store, on-line, or whatever other ways you get in touch with the customer. Customer experience includes all the interactions that take place between a company and its customers, and aren't just restricted to every day, basic transactions or service issues.

Companies that have traditionally delighted their customers such as; **John Lewis, First Direct, Southwest Airlines** and **Zappos**, seem to treat every interaction with a beguiling combination of enthusiasm, genuine emotion and proficiency, which for me are basic table stakes in the customer experience game. While not perfect and, as with many things, there is the occasional hiccup, these organizations will almost certainly have made enough deposits in their customer delight account to offset the odd customer service transgression, especially if there is a prompt acknowledgement and genuine apology – as opposed to the butt clenching, insincere, meaningless 'goodwill gesture' phrase trotted out by the **Ryanair's, BT's** and **British Gas'** of the world.

It's just that the bar has been set so incredibly low by the escalating frustration that we endure from most of the companies that we do business with every day, that we find we'd settle for *any* experience that quickly releases us from their clutches.

We're not talking about an occasional interaction. All of us probably have at least 5-10 business dealings a day that include a service element and, while *easy* should be the operative word, is there any reason why we shouldn't strive for, or expect, something that makes both parties (the customer and the employee) feel good and win?

The point is that we're happy if a *service* experience is effortless, but the Full Monty that is a customer experience needs to include much more than that. We could all use a little delight in our lives, being wowed and pleasantly surprised every now and then. Most of us are tired of being forgotten in long phone queues, let down by poor websites, and misunderstood by disinterested or powerless customer service agents

I've yet to be involved in a serious customer experience project where one of the key starting points didn't involve taking a long, hard and sometimes self-flagellating look at what the current customer experience delivery looked like, and that always means a return to the starting line. In my view, that line is drawn and intersects with our four fundamental principles that will establish a solid foundation for any part of the business, and are non-negotiable necessities in improving customer experience. Regardless of whether you measure delight, effort or ease of doing business, at some point you will need to drill down into the root causes of customer perceptions: what specific technologies, business processes and/or employee behaviours made doing business with the company easy or difficult? And what are the underlying principles or obstacles that created that result? Without these answers, a measure of effort (or ease of doing business) will not be very actionable. And if it does not drive actions, or isn't based on these four fundamental principles that improve the customer experience, what is the point of capturing effort, or any other measure?

So by all means please ensure that the repetitive, transactional, humdrum things that I need from you on a regular basis are so mind-numbingly easy, I can do it in my sleep.

When that happens – I'll be delighted!

What do you mean is Customer Experience Working?

Alright, we're getting a handle on who our customers are, and what they want, and where some of our challenges lie. We're delivering great customer service and getting great scores. So job done! Now what? With customer experience apparently becoming a global phenomenon, saying that it isn't working might be as popular as saying there's no Santa Claus. Every day I'm drowning in a sea of emails exhorting me to tune into this webinar, come to this seminar or read the 50 top tips about the value and importance of customer experience despite all the hype, for, customer experience isn't working - Yet. Don't get me wrong, as a customer, I'd love to see it happen. I'd be delighted if customer experience, as seen in many corporate press releases, annual reports, internet blogs and viral videos, and the ideas that evolve from it, became much more of a reality and actually made a difference. But they haven't, at least not for me as a customer.

Customer Service and Customer Experience – What's the difference?

Many businesses use various metrics to measure customer service as seen through the customers' eyes, including Net Promoter Scores (NPS) and Customer Satisfaction (CSAT). In doing this, they create a false dawn that all is well because customers give them good scores. While the concept and associated values of delivering great customer service are important, this is only one element of customer engagement for the overall customer experience, and is often necessary because something else in the customer journey has gone wrong, or the customer is demonstrably dissatisfied.

The term customer experience, describing the full life cycle spectrum of a customer's dealings with a company, is a relatively new one, and draws from a diverse range of disciplines and touchpoints, including customer service. The received corporate wisdom appears highly supportive of the strategic value of customer experience, but paradoxically, perhaps because it has been so thoroughly dissected, redefined, serenaded and written about, it's become financially exhausting and culturally contradictory as a viable strategy. Many businesses are now claiming that Customer

Experience is becoming increasingly impotent or a synonym for "It's too hard, too expensive, or too difficult to evaluate."

A recent survey by eConsultancy suggests that customer experience may indeed have hit the buffers. The survey showed that 40% of organizations cite 'complexity' as the greatest barrier to improving multichannel customer experience. And despite all the hype, the survey also confirms that only 26% of companies have a well-developed strategy in place for improving customer experience.

So, maybe we need to take a step or two back in order to move forward, and then see what is stopping many businesses from translating their customer experience dreams into an operational reality. I firmly believe that for many businesses, the issue of complexity, and the confusing melange of information about training, technology and process improvement et al, can be a barrier to getting started. Consequently, for those organizations that are in customer experience denial, or are sceptical about the payoff, finding a simpler but equally effective fundamental approach, is perhaps the most critical element of implementing a successful customer experience strategy.

Simplify, Simplify, Simplify

Simplifying has been valuable currency for many years. While it's had its share of detractors, it has also had many proponents. Henry David Thoreau may have been an early adopter of customer experience when he said, "Our life is frittered away by detail. Simplify, simplify, simplify." And Leonardo da Vinci, no slouch in the forward thinking department, summed it up nicely for the cool brands when he said, "Simplicity is the ultimate sophistication."

As with any worthwhile enterprise however, simplifying isn't always simple! There is no difference in the shiny new world of customer experience. The cacophony of noise that trumpets the importance of customer journey mapping, 'voice of the customer' surveys, employee engagement, making it easy, and the available latest whizzy technology often confuses, confounds and overwhelms even the most conscientious inhabitant of Planet Simple.

Principles still rule

While many of the processes and activities associated with the operational side of customer experience are undeniably important, necessary and effective, they are rarely the ideal starting point in building an effective customer experience strategy. Companies that seek to improve customer experience will not succeed unless they incorporate fundamental principles that govern human effectiveness and conscious thought. These principles are common to societies that prosper and endure, and are vital to establish a foundation for the tools and practices that transform an organization and bring a customer experience strategy to life.

I've long been a fan of the late Stephen Covey and have drawn much inspiration from his seminal tome *The 7 Habits of Highly Effective People*. The main theme, among a plethora of life changing ideas and highly visionary concepts, is that there are principles we must follow; natural laws in the human dimension that are just as real, just as unchanging as the laws in the physical dimension, such as gravity and motion.

One of Covey's simple yet highly effective examples is that of a farmer, who decides to take most of the summer off and then, in a flurry of activity in September, plants his fields hoping to fast track his crop by October. As Covey says "The farm is a natural system. The price must be paid and the process followed. You always reap what you sow, there is no shortcut."

The 'Sage of Omaha', Warren Buffet, has also brought his wisdom to the table noting that "No matter how great the talent or the efforts, some things just take time. You can't produce a baby in one month by making nine women pregnant."

Customer Experience reflects many of the important aspects of the human dimension, and can quite often run the gamut of emotions and reactions in a single 10 minute interaction. Yet despite this, few organizations have invested the time needed to look in the appropriate mirror to understand 'how' and 'why' a specific event unfolded as it did. I don't mean recording a call, or a contact centre side-by-side. I'm talking about the basic underlying human character traits that defined the outcome, both practical and emotional and its effect, good, bad or ugly, on the participants.

While customer experience may not be quite a natural system like farming; cutting corners, short term fixes and ignoring fundamental principles are equally likely to result in failure. These poorly disguised 'strategies', equally at home on the farm and known colloquially as putting 'lipstick on the pig', are as the name suggests, just a cosmetic exercise. This usually shows up as money and effort spent on marketing programs, new product announcements, corporate rebranding and customer service makeovers, without first having made sure that there is alignment with the underlying processes that focussed on the fundamental principles that drove and sustained long term, internal business transformation with evidential improvement.

And despite the increased focus on self-service, digital transformation, Artificial Intelligence (AI), Bots and other robotic initiatives, real customer engagement improvement can't exist or be sustained without the human touch at all levels, and in every role across the company.

The good news? Most people will consistently resist any attempt at making them officious, functional or anything other than caring sharing human beings. Let's check in with them and see how they're doing.

5. Now it's Personal – Just be you, the customers will love it

"Where there's officialism every human relationships suffers" - E.M. Forester

We'd only been in the restaurant about three minutes, but had already had some humorous and warm conversations with three of the staff who immediately made us feel both welcome and pleased that we'd chosen their restaurant in downtown Vancouver. What came through loud and clear was that these people were authentic in both their attitude and desire to make us feel at home, and although this was their 'job' , they treated us like friends and family and weren't simply just going through the motions.

Perhaps this wasn't that much of a stretch in a restaurant, (well at least not in Canada), but it doesn't always happen as naturally as this. Often, especially when they're reading their list of specials, it can sound robotic and more than a little scripted, especially when it's that special favourite, "Hi, my name is Bruce and I'll be your server today," (sorry if your name is Bruce!)

Proud to Serve – Happy to Help

As I'm quite often in Vancouver and have written frequently about my customer experiences there, I've come to expect this level of service. And, as this visit coincided with Canada being named #2 for Customer Service in a Zendesk poll, I wanted to really see what was in the magic sauce and who was cooking it.

This particular visit coincided with some positive reviews from a few friends who had experienced great customer service in Canada, and who wondered if they were lucky, or if this was the norm. I suggested that it was the latter and that the characteristics of this service were underpinned by the well-known Canadian values such as pride, tolerance and enthusiasm. In general most Canadians are proud to serve others, and don't see it as a menial or a temporary job between acting gigs. As a result, many Canadian companies have created an environment where employee engagement is a living, breathing organism, and participation in decisions is de rigueur. Pride in their company shines through and is reflected in their interactions with all their customers and guests.

Have a Nice Day – We really mean it!

Europeans often mock North Americans,' "Have a nice day" attitude as disingenuous. My friend and CX colleague Ian Golding wrote an interesting blog, coincidently entitled *"Have a nice day"*, in which he described his experiences on a trip to the USA, and wondered if they were really better at CX than the rest of the world. His conclusion was that they weren't. However, there were significant extremes in the quality of their interactions and many fell into the bucket of being accessible, functional and 'just doing their job.' For the most part people in Canada really mean it.

In Vancouver they keep it fresh and meaningful with genuine excitement and healthy dose of youthful creativity, open-mindedness and enthusiasm; it must be the mountains and the sea air. And nowhere is that more apparent than in its ever-burgeoning food and drink scene. Certainly the hospitality industry in Vancouver specifically, and Canada generally, is alive and well and is the place where many visitors get up close and personal with authentic and memorable customer service experiences.

Be yourself – Everyone else is already taken

But this latest restaurant visit, including the other positive experiences during my trip and the Zendesk survey, made me realize that there was something else. It appeared another equally critical element that continually freshens the offering and makes the moment more meaningful keeps people coming back for more. This was something that went deeper and wasn't just <u>in</u> the DNA of the people that delivered this great service, it <u>was</u> the DNA! It was the people being allowed to be themselves, to be real human beings and consequently provide a more authentic, consistent and memorable customer experience.

And this isn't just true for restaurants. Any business that truly cares about customers must allow their front line employees to express their own personalities, act naturally and spontaneously and by doing this, engage with the customer emotionally as well as practically.

Most of us naturally want to help others and come pre-wired with an attitude and a caring side that is ideally suited to achieving that objective. The best companies enhance their customer engagement by encouraging employees to build on these natural feelings and attitudes, and then let them loose on their customers, fellow employees and anyone within real or metaphorical hugging distance!

I was glad to see that I wasn't alone in my feelings when I read an article by Steven Van Belleghem entitled *"Defining the 'human touch' in the customer relationship."* While the article focuses primarily on the difference between human and computer based customer service interactions, Steven's underlying theme looks at three areas in which humans excel. This is their ability to add empathy, creativity and passion to any interaction. He notes that "Creativity and innovation are uniquely human characteristics. It is smart for companies to allow human creativity to blossom in all phases of the customer relationship. You must allow all your staff to think creatively about improvements that can benefit the customer."

I'm sure there will be people who will say there are risks associated with letting people unleash their personalities, creativity, or rich and fruity vocabulary on poor unsuspecting customers. However the alternative is to bore your customers with monotone agents who can't deviate from a script, have the personality of a turnip, and force customers into seeking other places to do business.

I'm not talking about thoughtless, knee-jerk or unplanned communications. This is all about giving employees permission to engage with customers on an emotional and personal level. It puts the responsibility for greater customer experience back where it belongs; in the hands, or voice, of the people who deliver the service. Let them have the knowledge needed, the trust and freedom to use it wisely, and set them free to execute.

Ditch the scripts – Act Naturally

But this isn't such a revolutionary idea. A recent survey from _Software Advice_, a website that provides information on customer support software, is a great illustration of the fact that most customers would prefer not to engage with agents who sounded as if they were reading from a script. Their survey - _What Customers Really Think About Your Call Center Script_ - had a lead-off question that really hit the nail on the head when it asked, "Does it improve your call experience when the customer service agent doesn't sound like they're reading from a script?" The response was a resounding "Yes" from 69% of respondents.

The survey was very enlightening and went on to focus on a number of other strategies. It discovered that using some of the very basic, human, unscripted, natural responses such as 'please' and 'thank you' were vastly more effective in building empathy, consistency and understanding into the interactions. And the reason for this seems equally simple. When agents say 'please' and 'thank you', they are not reading those words directly from a script, they're saying them naturally. They fit into normal, everyday dialogue, and the inflection and tone of the words are exactly how it should be.

I realize that many organizations have legal and regulatory statements that need to be covered. But I've worked with many organizations who have found innovative and natural ways to introduce these into the conversation, and meet their commitments, without reducing the customer to tears. If you want to see this in action check out the South West Airlines videos of various cabin crew announcements, where the passengers are reduced to tears – of laughter! I've also experienced this on WestJet in Canada and their flight attendants are equally engaging and humorous and clearly demonstrate that it's not just 'what' you say, it's 'how' you say it.

Put the spotlight on talent and let the feelings shine through

Engaged and trusted employees naturally want to help and find it easy to draw on their reserves of empathy and understanding, tune into their customer and turn up their performance. Forward thinking organizations put the spotlight on these talents and believe that if you can unleash imagination, encourage innovation and build trust, based on simple human behaviour and principles, then people will come together in a common purpose – and customers, employees and companies all win.

For those companies that truly understand this and measure success by the daily performance of the people who are the company, the results are clear. Not only are they reputationally and financially more profitable, but their employees achieve greater success and satisfaction in their work and life. They are also typically less likely to leave and more inclined to establish a career for the longer term.

As Steven Van Belleghem notes "Companies need to realize that in future the human element will be one of their scarcest resources in the customer relationship - and therefore one of the most strategically important. People love other people." It's only natural!

But companies can't make people be themselves or change their personalities, and individuals are still the best creators of great customer experiences by bringing the human touch to their interactions. Much of this is down to attitude. So where does that attitude come from?

Forget BYOD – BYOA is coming to a company near you!

As mobile technology marches on unrelentingly, and many device owners appear to be surgically or unnaturally attached to their smartphones and tablets, the concept of Bring Your Own Device (BYOD) has gained significant currency. Briefly stated, BYOD refers to the policy of permitting employees to bring personally owned mobile devices (laptops, tablets, and smart-phones) to their workplace, and to use those devices to access privileged company information and applications. In many cases this also means they can actually do their jobs more effectively, efficiently and from any location. Although this latter capability is still an anathema to the many companies stuck in the seventies, who don't trust their employees, especially when it comes to customer service roles.

BYOA makes more sense – It's cheaper and it comes pre-installed

But for me, a much better idea, that comes with similar benefits, that is less costly and great for all companies regardless of sizes and types, is BYOA – Bring Your Own Attitude. And the customer service world where I spend much of my time is a perfect and timely breeding ground for BYOA.

So what is BYOA, and why does it have a place in today's business world? There's no questioning the fact that a great attitude is a fundamental, important and enduring asset for any employee to have in any business. And if you're young, but come with a great attitude and enthusiasm pre-installed, as many do, then that can overcome lack of experience, company knowledge and other skills that can be learned as you progress. But why doesn't this happen naturally in the world of customer service? Wanting to help others, especially those that clearly are in need of assistance and support, would seem to be a perfectly natural and worthy thing to do. Most of us, when confronted with this situation in a personal circumstance with relatives, friends and even strangers –think of the Good Samaritan – don't hesitate to step in.

The times they are a'changin

For some time now I've been evangelizing the need to encourage more of this new breed of employees to consider customer service, not just as a stop-gap measure or job between acting gigs, but as a worthwhile, fulfilling career.

One of the main reasons is that I feel strongly how the nature and future of work is changing – a theme explored in much more detail by Alison Maitland and Peter Thomson in their excellent book *Future Work*. This looks at how Millennials, Gen Y and Digital Natives are not content with the status quo, either as customers or prospective employees, and want change - now. These new employees, with their focus on work-life balance and desire for an experience – not a job – are changing the rules, and the game, for good.

Leave your personality at the door

It's an unfortunate reality that many businesses, especially those with customer service contact centres establish an inflexible, policy driven, scripted approach to customer interactions. As a result, and in a drive to only meet company focused metrics, they discourage employees from bringing their personality and their positive and caring attitude into the equation. The result is often dis-engaged, dis-interested employees that deliver inconsistent performances and are constantly in 'seeking new challenges' mode.

BYOA is a winning combination and everyone plays a part

However, success with BYOA isn't just down to the employee's attitude. It needs a fertile and frequently nourished environment, created by businesses and business leaders that see beyond profit at all costs and eschew mind numbing, senseless company policies and procedures. **John Lewis**, **Metro Bank** and **Autoglass®** are living breathing examples of where everyone comes together for the common good, and where personality and attitude are allowed to thrive and flourish.

Another business that consistently provides me with evidence of BYOA in action is **Holiday Inn,** and their Colliers Wood property in South London, which is our home away from home when travelling to London. The poster children for BYOA are their front of house team, who always greet us with a smile and recognition when we check in. The hotel management has assembled a great team whose welcoming, friendly, smiling faces are all part of their DNA and not optional extras. But it's not just this part that keeps us coming back. At any one time all of the team chip in to do whatever is necessary, beyond their actual role, to ensure a great guest experience. There's no "Not my job, man," here. This is where BYOA can really shine and where doing the right thing for the guest, or customers, just comes naturally.

Another business that I've been fortunate to learn more about, and where they hire for attitude and educate for knowledge, is **Screwfix Direct** in Yeovil, Somerset. Their contact centre has frequently been recognized at a number of contact centre and customer service awards. They've won recognition for individual and team achievements and, it's evident that there is a culture where enthusiasm, willingness, adaptability, along with determination and a high level of competence make the difference. You can't just pick that up at a customer experience conference or on a technology webinar.

It should come naturally – But in case it doesn't

Clearly there needs to be some boundaries but, as with many things in life, most of us in polite society know instinctively how to interact courteously and respectfully towards our fellows and don't need rules for fundamental, day to day activities. It's often been said that people buy from people and that's never been truer than today. We all crave the human touch, regardless of how many shiny new toys technology companies try to convince us that we need. As my friend, fellow human being and customer experience aficionado Maz Iqbal said in a recent blog "The focus is almost exclusively on the technical stuff (metrics, data, analytics, technology, processes) and almost no recognition of the human."

But that doesn't mean that BYOA always comes naturally to every employee, or is fully developed, or encouraged at every company. Companies still need to find innovative and creative ways to bring this talent to life. I've created company-wide workshops and initiatives with themes such as *Bringing your Inner Customer to Life - Unleashing the Power of your Positive Personality* that can do much to enhance and further develop these natural capabilities.

These workshops are designed to help people and companies that are already on the right track, and are new learning initiatives aimed at bringing out the best of their best, to inspire, engage and enhance their natural attitude, and have a positive impact on customers and other colleagues. This is yet another example of the importance of aligning and engaging the organization in a common purpose and ensuring that everyone gets the memo. So let's take another trip.

6. Crossing the Great Divide – Organizational Engagement Brings Customer Experience to Life

"Across the great divide, Just grab your hat, and take that ride" – Robbie Roberston

There is a magical location in the Canadian Rockies, north of Calgary known as the Continental Divide, or the Great Divide. It's where rivers drain and then separate to flow to the opposite sides of the continent. The outflow literally ends up oceans apart, in the Atlantic, Arctic or Pacific. Each of those destinations has their own geographic, cultural and reputational personalities. This, as any visitor will tell you, results in extraordinarily different and unique experiences.

Business differences that divide but don't conquer

Many businesses today have their own Great Divide, especially when it comes to customer engagement and customer experience strategy. These aren't just great divisions, but yawning chasms of diverse thought, conflicting ideas and varying departmental agendas, stretching across the business. This is often characterized by divergent views on what the corporate priorities should be, and where the customer fits into that debate.

Is process more important than outcomes? Is the customer really at the heart of all they do, or just a slick marketing slogan? Do they follow their technology head or customer experience heart? While these issues can flow through any department in a company, differences of opinion and direction between IT and the customer service team often produce the biggest headlines – and headaches. This is typically the battleground where these skirmishes play out, but are these groups really two solitudes, and always strange bedfellows, or can they be united in purpose and aligned in strategy to generate positive outcomes?

In today's multi-dimensional and digitally driven world, a customer's attitude toward a business, beyond products and services, has many defining influences. These can be a combination of their previous interactions, moments of truth and desperation with staff, and other experiences of varying quality. But generally, will not be entirely based on a single, process-influenced contact event or technology failure.

That said, if the event is particularly memorable for the wrong reasons: long hold time, confusing self-service menu, incorrect customer data, poorly functioning website or app, rude, unhelpful or knowledge deficient staff, then the technology and other associated and contributing elements will stand out and be the focus of criticism and negative customer feedback. This is very often the case when an organization uses touchpoint Net Promoter Scores (tNPS) to assess each discrete interaction and where the customer has a short memory that only reflects how they felt at a particular moment, or with the attitude of a particular individual.

Organizational Engagement is more than a marriage of convenience

There is a lot of positive noise about the importance of high quality customer and employee engagement, and with good reason. These are key planks in building a successful customer experience stage and putting on a great performance. There is, however, another piece of the foundation that is becoming increasingly more valuable in supporting the overall strategy: That is **Organizational Engagement**.

To successfully engage employees, provide customers with an outstanding experience and create a high performance culture, businesses need to be fully aligned and develop organizational engagement that is more than just lip service or a hastily contrived tactical shotgun marriage between departments. Companies that fail to do this typically have negative customer outcomes, increased attrition, endless internal finger pointing, reputational damage and disappointing financial results.

This foundational element can span myriad activities and touch all parts of the business. One of the most valuable procedural items is the ability to address many of the challenges that organizations have with lines of business operating in a common purpose to achieve the transformation required to be a truly customer centric company. A key component in this process is to start with a new company-wide collaboration agreement, or social contract. This features operational agility, departmental flexibility, and a new level of mutual understanding that can't be formulated at a single meeting, or articulated in a glib corporate slogan.

Strong relationships with customers, employees, business partners, shareholders and with society must be reflected in business strategy. Organisations must create an operating environment that supports its internal relational achievement, as well as having employees that are engaged in a culture that enables them to deliver it. And yet, recent research from *Forbes* showed that while 65% of organisations have an agreed strategy, only 14% of employees fully understand it, and unsurprisingly, as a result less than 10% of organisations successfully execute their strategy. In other words, failing to ambulate their rhetoric, perhaps better known as 'not walking the talk'.

Cut out the turf wars – Start to grow the business organically

These agreements must contain clearly defined rules of engagement that transcend silos and turf wars, and truly gets to the heart of business issues that are measured in customer terms, and that all stakeholders can understand and act upon. How do departments such as IT balance operational metrics that have been their guiding light, and often their saving grace, with the new customer experience measures and outcome based results that are now grabbing corporate headlines? How about marketing and their holy grail of attracting new customers? What role do they have in retention? And how can finance help retrieve a customer that's about to kiss you goodbye?

Most businesses will claim to have their organizational act together. "We have regular meetings, don't we?" "We all subscribe to the 'customer is at the heart of all we do' charter." But, in a quiet corner of the saloon bar, perhaps with the temporary courage that a small whiskey can supply, I'm sure that you'll get a very different answer.

Building the bridges – Supporting the strategy

To help you cross your own Great Divide there are some key structural and operational foundations that are necessary to build the bridges that will support organizational engagement:

1. First, you must discover what and where the challenges lie to delivering a great customer experience, and the role and importance of a cross-functional approach to meeting them.

2. Then, it's vital to develop a greater understanding of where you want to go in terms of a realistic customer experience ambition. What's the destination and who are your internal and external travelling companions?

3. Next is the key planning phase to identify priorities, understand potential road-blocks, gain company-wide support and truly build a climate of organizational engagement that forms the basis for the social contract.

4. Finally, the development of the long term customer experience blueprint that enables you to foster innovation and creativity, while maintaining operational excellence and enhancing customer engagement.

For any business this means a well-documented, unambiguous, company-wide definition of what customer experience means. More specifically, agreement and direction on a true, achievable and measurable corporate vision, values and purpose that goes beyond a slick marketing slogan. This will also identify any gaps in people's understanding of, and the ability to execute, the vision, mission, objectives and strategic direction. It should include a road map that provides a framework for defining and benchmarking your differentiating, profitable customer experiences, and a time line for implementation.

Where you are in terms of interactions with customers based on external/internal feedback? What are the behaviours, skills, processes and supporting technology needed to support the vision? How can a clearly defined customer experience strategy, increase product holdings and/or overall profitability? It might seem like the right thing to do, but what does it take to execute? And how will we know if we get it right?

Finding your purpose and direction - Getting on the right path

This can be challenging, which is probably why many companies file this in the "It's too difficult" drawer. But one very effective action that forward thinking companies find less difficult, is getting the right people in the room for a no-holds-barred, honest, frank and truly introspective assessment of the organization. This can be a great launch pad for authentic engagement, but doesn't mean that everyone has to agree on every topic.

A free flowing and robust debate where differences of opinion can be celebrated and lead to Damascene moments and even Archemedic discoveries, are far more fruitful, liberating and entertaining. Seeking consensus will probably end up making you more friends, but potentially leaving you in the same state of inaction or inertia. Chatham House or Vegas rules are abandoned for the duration, as you really don't want it to stay there. However, verbatim transcripts may need some careful editing before being released into the wild. Despite my apparent cynicism about company meetings, this is definitely one I feel strongly that you should sign up to. I've been involved in a number of these as a facilitator and have seen some very positive outcomes that have led to development of some truly different and memorable customer experiences, and engaged colleagues.

Why Organizational Alignment is Important

- Colleagues will have a stronger, measurable understanding of the brand, your strategic vision, purpose and the value that the company brings and what it means to customers

- Company-wide agreement (but not necessarily consensus), support and development of a strong organizational appetite for, and adoption of, change and the way to enable it

- Creation and management of a prioritized list of top customer experience improvements that involves a senior executive accountable for implementation and measurement

- Identification of barriers to success inherent in people, process and technology components

- Establishment of a balanced and realistic list of high-impact actions and quick wins

- Increased visibility of, and participation in, the customer experience strategy by all colleagues that will increase advocacy, keep the program alive and embedded in your company culture

- Alignment of business goals with customer-focused culture that can form the basis for a customer experience blue print

- Development of measures that can provide clear evidence of customer experience impact as a criterion for all business and investment decisions

Success in this initiative doesn't mean everyone is on the same page, but it's useful to be reading from the same book, and clearly there has to be some coming together. Cohesion of sprit and a non-destructive collision of ideas can lead to continual and measurable progress.

The operative word in all of this is engagement, as in any human endeavour to bring people together. It means making a connection with those with whom you have more in common that you may think, and where the outcome is mutually beneficial. This is 'when' and 'where' real conversations can take place, practical ideas exchanged and where rather than being oceans apart, you're all sailing, or possibly bailing, together on a voyage of customer experience discovery. This voyage will potentially lead to a positive sea change in your business and the actions of the people that navigate its direction.

When you have everyone rowing in the same direction this also has a tremendous impact on your reputation, and in the vernacular of the times, your brand. While a positive, caring, empathetic attitude has many customer engagement benefits, the immediate and lasting impact that it can have on a company's brand are incalculable. Good or bad reviews, especially those in the travel and hospitality industries, often have their start from a human interaction. Your employees are the best and most frequently cited guardians, or destroyers of your brand and reputation. However, it doesn't take much to knock an oar or two out of the water, leading to that that sinking feeling that comes with 'brand overboard'.

7. A Brand-Aid Solution – If your name's on it make sure your heart's in it

Bandages and bad stuff tend to stick fast and are painful to remove – Gerry Brown

In 1961, a new motel opened in Toronto that was built by a young man with no experience in the hospitality business. The chosen location was on a street that had once been the site for politicians homes and the captains of industry.

By the sixties the residents were more likely to be ladies of negotiable affection, or those who sought solace in the bottom of a glass or at the end of a needle. Like any entrepreneur he dreamed of success, but he didn't have a grand plan or a vision of how it might all turn out. What he did have was a fundamental and enduring understanding of what customers would value. He knew the importance of forging close relationships with guests, employees and managers, and he also recognized the need for a strong foundation that would support and reinforce his business model. These became the four pillars of the organization's business model and his overriding philosophy; *quality, service, culture* and *brand*.

Foundational metaphors are used frequently in business. I've used them liberally in support of my own ideas about customers when I developed the *Four Principles of Customer Experience.* But this man was a builder by trade and this wasn't just a slick marketing slogan, but a key element and deeply entrenched and enduring belief in his transition to a hotelier.

His name is Isadore Sharp and his first property in Toronto, The Four Seasons Motel Hotel, was the start of a hospitality journey that led to the creation of a leading luxury hotel brand, with over 100 properties in 39 countries. The word 'brand', which features prominently in Isadore Sharp's business philosophy, really does mean something when used by the *Four Seasons*.

Own the brand - Deliver the experience

One of his earliest business decisions was to manage, rather than own those hotels, and to make service the brand's distinguishing edge. This meant that they controlled the promise and the experience under the brand. However, for many other hotels, that's just a logo to adorn their properties with and they can lean on until it bends or breaks. Many multi-national hotel companies 'own' the brand, but the operational delivery is the responsibility of a franchisee and this is where the problems start. The hotel company is great at developing slogans, crafting mission statements and making promises. But, when guests arrive at the hotel their experience as delivered by the franchisee often doesn't match the promise they expected.

I spoke earlier about Holiday Inn. This was the brain child of Kemmons Wilson, another young idealistic builder from Memphis, Tennessee. Started in 1951, in a golden era of family life and post-war aspirations, and aided by the development of a cross-country road network, more frequent leisure travel became the norm. Mr Wilson recognized the need for clean, reliable, affordable accommodation for young growing families who were his target market. His motto, and his promise, was "No surprises". It was a simple yet poignant symbol of value and expectation that all his employees understood and delivered daily. While the motto has checked out, the spirit and the promise remain, and Mr Wilson's original dream and value proposition survive and prosper.

While the company does have some luxury brands, such as Intercontinental, HUALUXE and Crowne Plaza, many of their properties are squarely aimed at the mid-low range market with their Holiday Inn and Holiday Inn Express brands. (This doesn't mean however, that the guest doesn't get great value). I stay there regularly, as I shared with you earlier, and am always positively surprised by the great service promise that lives on.

Everyone is in the customer experience business

Those of you who are frequent travellers will recognize that the quality and value of hotels are of a vital importance in making these trips less onerous. I'm continually reminded of this, particularly when I have a bad experience, or my friends share one on LinkedIn or Facebook. Most of the staff must have missed the memo about customer experience being everyone's responsibility. These bad reviews clearly demonstrate what can happen when brand value and service delivery is disconnected and separated from operational reality. This disconnection seems all too prevalent, and is often magnified at airport hotels where employees see the guests as purely transient, but then fail to see that it's not just a single room per night that's in jeopardy, but the life time value of a guest and their family who can become either brand advocates or bad news bearers based on a single poor experience. It is a consistent, sustained building of trust delivered by each employee that nurtures brand loyalty.

Bigger must be Better- the Fred Goodwin School of (mis)management

In my mind the overriding reason for a lack of consistency is the consolidation and mergers and acquisitions that have been prevalent across all businesses in recent years, especially in the hospitality sector. The most recent room sharing event occurred when *Starwood* was acquired by *Marriot*, thus forming the world's 'new' biggest hotel company. The various reports were littered with references to annual cost savings, being the uncontested top hotel player and increased shareholder value. It was topped off by *Marriot* CEO, Arne Sorenson, who said that he and his colleagues had "Become more impressed by what we can accomplish by being bigger." Things then went from bad to worse (for guests) when Daniel Lesser, CEO of *LW Hospitality Advisors*, (clearly one who worships at the altar of St Michael of O'Leary) wrote in *Hotels* magazine, "I firmly believe lodging owners and operators need to be more concerned with economic yields as compared with service and guest satisfaction." He was even more candid in another post: "I believe the lodging industry should nickel and dime the same population that flies and/or cruises." You'll notice that the guest or the customer doesn't figure in any of the reports or any of the statements, other than as the poor stiffs to be fleeced unapologetically.

In 2016, we saw another mega deal go south when Unilever wisely decided to resist the overtures from Kraft-Heinz, no doubt remembering the broken promises about keeping a key Cadbury factory open, and more recently the decision to abandon Cadbury's commitment to using Fairtrade cocoa beans to produce its chocolate. The best and final words were from a 'senior Unilever source' who said "We invest in brands to generate growth. They (Kraft) strip out costs and let the brands decline." I'm sure that John Cadbury would agree.

You might well call this the Fred Goodwin school of (mis)management, where bigger is always better, there's always another deal to be made, and greed trumps good business sense. This acquisitive behaviour rarely, if ever, benefits customers. It simply sates the avaricious, arrogant appetite, extravagant ego and unbridled corporate lust of the CEO or MD that sees it as their career defining moment.

Bringing the brand to life - Show them that you CARE

I strongly believe that the primary focus for a hotel, beyond a warm bed, should be a duty of care. Not so much in the health or social sense, though all of those responsibilities may well apply.

When you think about it about it, the traveller, especially those on business, are quite often alone, away from their loved ones, familiar surroundings, and perhaps are apprehensive or nervous about an important business meeting. Isadore Sharp certainly recognized this and notes in his excellent biographic book *Four Seasons – The story of a Business Philosophy,* that "This isn't about frills; this is about the services that you need to do business effectively, and that's what we're here to provide." This is the time that they need an actual or metaphorical arm around their shoulder. The former may not be listed in a hotel's services and perhaps strays dangerously into the area of whispered extras, but the property should recognize this need, and be able to deliver on the latter, as this is really at the heart of what a brand promise means. That may differ in its depth and breadth, depending on the brand position, but there are some fundamental principles that any property should follow and that can show your guests that you really CARE.

Consistency
Authenticity
Responsibility
Engagement

Consistency

The hotel business is awash with slogans and promises, but to deliver on them, and truly influence the culture of the organization, consistency is a non-negotiable cornerstone. Isadore Sharp notes that "The one idea that our customers value is the consistent quality of our exceptional service." This is where the hotels with disconnected teams and disengaged employees really fall down, and this isn't just the preserve of the luxury brands. Consistency is the hallmark of my *Holiday Inn* experiences that I featured in the previous chapter. At any one time all of the team chip in to do whatever is necessary, beyond their actual role, to ensure that we have a great guest experience. It is where doing the right thing for the guest or customers just comes naturally, and where enthusiasm, willingness, adaptability, along with determination and a high level of competence make the difference.

Authenticity

We all laugh at Basil Fawlty and his fawning and insincere efforts to curry favour with his guests on *Fawlty Towers*. Generally we can spot the impostors in most customer service situations. But we appreciate it when people are encouraged to be themselves; to be real human beings and consequently provide a more authentic, consistent and memorable customer experience. Brands are only authentic if the customer experience matches or exceeds the promises made in their communications. While recognizing *Four Seasons* is a hard to beat role model for exceptional service, there is also another strong contender in the sector – *Ritz Carlton Hotels*. Their motto is "Ladies and Gentlemen serving Ladies and Gentlemen." It wasn't dreamed up by anyone on Madison Avenue, but by a 14 year old boy named Horst Schulze in Germany. Now, he did go on to become the co-founder and president of Ritz Carlton, but he also ensured that this was at the heart of how their employees were treated and, in turn, delivered on the promise. While the leadership shares what they expect, they let the team members create what they needed to do for the guests. This is based on desired outcomes, not restrictive policies or procedures, which allows the employee to inject their own personality so that it becomes an authentic, honest and repeatable experience.

Responsibility

Bad things can happen with even the most customer focused businesses, and how people within those organizations respond is usually what stays in the mind of the customer long after the event. Very often when things go wrong, especially with train companies, airlines, mobile phone providers and banks, you usually get the lame "We apologize for any inconvenience caused, which has as much feeling as a frozen moose on a Canadian prairie in winter. The customer facing people are usually left to face the music from dissatisfied customers, and often have to explain frequent service failures or senseless policies and procedures emanating from faceless Senior Executives.

The reality is that they would truly like to fix the problem. Most of us naturally want to help others, and if left to our own devices would certainly do so. But as noted earlier, without the backing and commitment of the organization, many colleagues are left exposed and lack the empowerment and trust to put things right.

When employees are trusted to make the right decision – for the customer - even if they can't solve the problem immediately, the employee can own it and see it through to resolution. This is all about giving employees permission to engage with customers on an emotional and personal level. It puts the responsibility for great customer experience back where it belongs; in the hands or voice of the front line people who own the customer moment and deliver the service.

Engagement

Engaged and trusted employees naturally want to help and find it easy to locate their 'inner customer' where they store their reserves of empathy and understanding, to tune into their customer and turn up their performance. But engagement doesn't come easily or in quantity. A recent study from **Gallup** showed that the number of engaged employees worldwide continue to be less than 20%. Companies such as *Four Seasons, Ritz Carlton* and *Holiday Inn*, lead the way in customer experience and business success. While there may be differences in market segments, they've all based their culture of excellence on a strong set of core values, or a code of behaviour that is neither an empty promise nor a hastily devised marketing slogan. This is not mandated solely from above, but is based on shared beliefs, values, and practices. These companies understand that one of the key outputs from increased employee engagement is where all of the employees have a strong voice, are actively involved and are directly responsible for developing the fundamentals on which their service culture is built.

Howard Schultz from *Starbucks* nailed it when he said "Authentic brands don't emerge from marketing cubicles or advertising agencies. They emanate from everything the company does…"

I'll leave the final words on what a brand means to Isadore Sharp. "One way to characterise *Four Seasons'* service would be to call it an exchange of mutual respect performed with an attitude of kindness."

His heart, and those of his staff, will always be in it.

8. Technology's the answer, now what was the question?

"I don't need absolution, just a simple solution will do" - Jimmy Buffet, Coastal Confessions

Define your vision, align your strategy and create your roadmap

As the customer experience bandwagon picks up speed, even more passengers clamber aboard eager to step up to the bar and drink from what they think is the flowing fountain of endless IT expenditure. These arrivistes are many of the technology companies, some of whom found ways to incorporate 'customer experience' into their names or mission statements, which, as you can probably figure out, didn't allow for much creativity or innovation. In addition to borrowing CX for their own purposes, these organizations have also thrown Digital Transformation (DT) into the mix to attract prospects into their demo labs for displays of the latest technological wizardry. As a result this can lead to digital capabilities being developed in isolation, in a dark room and without input from customers or front line colleagues.

However, what many businesses discovered, or have known for some time, is that while technology is an important enabling element, it's not the natural starting point to make CX a reality in the business. David Radburn, Head of IT at Caffè Nero said "While you need to understand the tech well enough to challenge your software vendors, the most important thing is to understand the business.

Being too techie can stop you focusing on the right things." This isn't new news. Over a hundred years ago Henry David Thoreau noted "Our inventions are wont to be pretty toys, which distract our attention from serious things. They are but improved means to an unimproved end."

To make CX come alive and stay top of mind in your organization, it's vital that you address cultural, procedural and other business challenges that will slow down the speed of your transformation, unless you give them the time and attention they deserve. Especially when it comes to defining and deploying the digital experience that your customers want and expect. CX links organizations to customers at emotional, operational and physiological levels, and all of these need to be fully explored to provide a clear, company-wide understanding of your CX strategy and a blueprint for executing it. Without that, digital transformation may only be sexy apps, whizzy websites and a chat bot named Gladys.

Doing this in a truly collaborative environment will help to develop the guiding principles and uncover a clear connection between the digital framework and the broader customer engagement and the CX imperatives that drive them. It will also provide the organization with a road map that has been plotted on strong multi-departmental and customer experience principles. Without this alignment you will not be able to truly connect your customers to your business to deliver the immediacy, value and relevance they want and need in their interactions with you. It will also be a triumph of style over substance.

Digital Transformation – Hype or Hope?

With organizations falling over themselves in the race to become 'digital' and using that as a key element to improve customer experience, it feels blasphemous to cast aspersions at the concept or to ask 'why'. But perhaps the question isn't 'why', but 'how' and possibly 'when' and 'where'. The latter questions have their provenance in the fact that while there is probably no C-level debate about the validity of a digital agenda, it's less clear as to how to establish the priorities for the vision, and to agree on a logical starting point. Marketing, sales, ecommerce and probably others will all state the case for "Me first." And these conflicting ambitions and opinions can put the brakes on any DT project as organizational turf wars break out. Perhaps though there is a solution, or at least a workable approach that can address the needs of various stakeholders, while at the same time establishing a flexible, cross company strategy and deploying a solid physical platform.

There's legacy and then there's legacy

This initiative has its provenance in some of the issues that many companies are facing as they begin their digital journey. An effective digital strategy can drive enhanced customer contact across channels and devices, and then connect both internal and external stakeholders to improve most aspects of business and positively impact customer experience. However, complex multi-solution integration slows time-to-market, burns investment budgets, and often leaves cross-company teams frustrated with the outcomes. While various new customer interaction solutions can provide point-to-point integration, they often don't meet the requirements of multi-functional business teams. In particular integration with myriad back-end legacy systems can deprive them of the business value of digital services and drive up the costs and time to implement.

Great historical figures that perform daring deeds, live exemplary and inspirational lives or make massive contributions to humankind are rightly feted in history books, statues, buildings and other visible signs of their time on earth. However, they also leave something less tangible, but more memorable and lasting which is a *legacy* that carries on and reminds us of what they achieved during their lifetimes. It is also something that is measurably and visibly powerful that inspires and informs subsequent generations. While most of us probably won't find a lasting place in any future history books, the idea of leaving a legacy for our children and our families, whether that is financial or reputational, is something most of us can identify with and strive for.

In the business world many personal legacies are less memorable and more toxic, and deserve to be consigned to the Rip Off Rascals Hall of Shame. The Enron gang, Robert Maxwell, and Fred Goodwin immediately come to mind, but there is one definition of legacy that many companies would also probably like to forget, but are reminded of every day by their customers and employees.

This is their old and creaking technology defined in many dictionaries as "Of, relating to, or being a previous or outdated computer system." As a customer the big clue is when a customer service agent says, "My system's slow" followed by the even more awful, "Bear with me." In the contact centre agents are doing a lot of cutting, pasting, toggling, swearing and then leaving, usually in that order. I've certainly witnessed the frustration and embarrassment that colleagues feel that comes with slow, cumbersome legacy systems, when what the customer really wants is effortless, fast and effective service.

Crossing the Digital Divide- The fast train is on platform one

It's becoming clear that to successfully traverse this potential minefield, organizations must adopt a digital experience framework and integration mind-set with the capability to address these challenges. While newer, nimble interaction solutions can provide fast access to customer data, there's another key element that brings it all together. Customer critical digital strategies typically rely heavily on Application Programming Interfaces (APIs) and/or digital experience platforms, to deliver the robust and flexible integration they need that can connect content, data, and systems to unify marketing, commerce, and service processes over multiple touchpoints.

A recent report from Forrester Research summarizes this nicely by stating that "APIs are perhaps the most critical technology in digital business design." Gartner have equally strong feelings and say "It is impossible to provide the platform for any digital strategy without full life cycle API management."

Many businesses have done the hard yards in engaging employees, eliminating senseless policies and procedures, developing a meaningful purpose and building a customer centric culture. But, despite all of this, they still struggle to deliver consistently on customer expectations as the underlying or enabling technology is often not fit for purpose, and further conspires to negate all the positive feelings and activities. Now is the hour to hook up to the Silicon Valley drip and slowly start the flow of innovation and activation coursing through your business. Yes, it's time to say goodbye to some of the old faithful legacy retainers, or at least to give them a bit of a rest, and lovingly embrace the newest shiny toys that will actually make a difference. All this in the right hands and on the right platform, become valuable and irreplaceable tools of the trade.

Paradoxically, many of these legacy systems still have value and actually do much of the corporate heavy lifting whilst performing valiant and important tasks involving a wide range of applications. Unfortunately they seldom do them quickly, easily or elegantly, leaving many to curse about the "Damned legacy system." Using sporting analogies, you can think of them as the linemen in American Football, or the front row in rugby that do all the unseen donkey work while the quarterbacks, running backs and fly halves who dance speedily around and through them on their way to the big scores and equally large headlines and pay packets.

Your best legacy may be in the cloud

But, as in sports, there is a new breed of solutions that are fleet of foot, able to turn on a dime and have all the flexibility of a yogi on speed, and that are breathing new life and purpose into legacy systems. Especially when they team up with API or Digital Experience platforms. They also leave the customers and colleagues cheering them on enthusiastically while not costing businesses Premier or Major League transfer fees and wages.

These solutions are not meant to be immediate replacements for legacy systems, although many are able to perform some of their functions very capably. But, along with integration platform are the critical first steps for companies seeking to crawl out from under the train wreck that is increasingly complex, expensive and inflexible legacy IT solutions and dependent on bloated, self-serving and increasingly archaic IT departments. They can play a huge supporting role in mediating between systems to fetch and carry the data and information required to quickly and accurately address customer inquiries. The challenge that most businesses face is information and customer data that resides in different places and in different forms - usually in the much maligned legacy systems that is expensive to replace or modify.

As I noted in Chapter 3, the solutions that address this challenge most effectively are usually cloud based interaction platforms that can provide immediate, updated and visual access to customer history, regardless of channel, and are integrated within a single window that can access the legacy big boys when necessary. These are fast becoming the solution of choice for many businesses, large or small, and the agility, flexibility of both the solutions and the companies providing them can decreases risk, deployment time frames and the overall investment.

It isn't my aim in this book to take you on an extensive tour of the various technologies available, but one of the key benefits of cloud technology is that you can return to 'best of breed' solutions, as integration is becoming far simpler and less costly. The end result is that these solutions can make life easier, quicker and satisfying for customers, smoother and less time consuming for colleagues and more cost effective for the business. Now that's a legacy and something to really remember you by!

Now, let's see if I can leave a legacy for you by starting our journey with the Four Principles.

9. Building the Foundation –
The Four Principles

"By centering our lives on correct principles, we create a solid foundation for development" - Stephen Covey

I realize that building the foundation usually happens early in any worthy initiative. But I hope that the journey so far has still been relevant and valuable, as well as providing insight into the history, the mystery and the reality of why CX is important.

When it came to understanding more about how, where and why CX was so effective and important, I looked closer at some of the companies that really do have customer experience working for them, and found strong evidence of the *Four Principles* that we met earlier and that are vital to the development and sustainability of a Customer Experience program. Just as a reminder these are; **Culture, Commitment, Community and Communication.** The power of these principles, both individually and in combination, is that they are founded on deep, basic truths that have broad and enduring applications. When integrated into our daily lives they provide a context and a framework that can mobilize people to develop the understanding, skills and patience to handle almost any situation. This is what it takes to bring home the bacon and is way beyond 'lipstick on the pig'. You can't pick these up at the cosmetic counter.

These Four Principles are simple and each is intentionally represented by just a single word that very much mirrors the important and real life values, and how we approach the world as individuals. They can be, and are, used by all of us every day in our interactions with others; when we hold open doors, support worthy causes, apologize unreservedly and sometimes unnecessarily (in the UK and Canada) and (occasionally) smile at strangers. In a customer service environment you really can't make people do what they don't want to do, or at least you can't do it indefinitely or with everyone. Any discussion involving principles and natural law will undoubtedly uncover a full complement of ideas and concepts that can apply to almost any eventuality. While we may all have slightly different interpretations of these specific principles, I also believe that there is universal awareness and understanding of their value, their relevance and their importance to the survival and growth of any business.

Let's look closer and see how these principles relate to, and inspire, our customer experience journey.

1. Culture

Culture, especially customer-focused corporate culture, isn't something you can mandate, although that hasn't stopped many CEOs from trying. Without a customer-focused culture, organizations can never truly achieve a strong customer experience. It's often the missing element for companies that continue to lose the plot when it comes to customer experience. Your culture is effectively the bedrock of your company. It is a set of shared beliefs, values, and practices that is developed from the inside out and based on additional, complimentary principles such as fairness, courtesy and empathy. The key word here is 'shared', and by doing that you create an environment where it is real, actionable and constantly under review. Businesses that continue to be successful financially, reputationally and have a strong ethical workforce have almost assuredly done it by involving everyone in the endeavour. Just like other life affirming actions, corporate culture is very much founded on a discipline and a set of behaviours and skills that are defined, refined and guarded by the very people responsible for delivery on the company's customer promises. Jack Ewing notes in his book *Faster, Higher, Farther*, "Corporate culture is never written down; it's just what everyone knows."

While, as I noted, culture can't be mandated, it does need authentic leadership and support from the top to really make it sustainable and reflective of the organization's values and purpose. This doesn't just mean a snappy corporate video with the CEO telling everyone that "Customers are at the heart of everything we do", although visible, constant reminders are important. An environment where the senior leadership is consistently engaged and actively model the attitudes and behaviours the company expects from the whole company in alignment with the values and hard won reputation. To quote Jack Ewing again, "Employees will not always do what is right, that it's up to management to set an example."

Setting that example and engaging the whole company can take many forms, but, as with many things, frequent, honest two-way communication is a key element to ensure vigilance and ongoing awareness of customer and colleague issues that can signal any negative shift in culture. The key elements are having employees that are both encouraged and rewarded for identifying customer issues, and senior managers who share company decisions and direction that can be influenced and informed by employee feedback and intervention.

I've recently seen posts and comments on social media suggesting that businesses shouldn't necessarily model themselves on successful companies such as Amazon, Apple, John Lewis and other customer experience stalwarts. While I recognize that Joe Bloggs Plumbing may have different challenges from the 'big boys', this doesn't mean that there aren't lessons to be learned, ideas and innovation to be tested. After all, the recipients of the services from businesses, large and small, are all still people like us.

When you first rally the troops and start down the principle path in your initial cross-functional team meeting, there are two simple exercises to help you to get a strong sense of the current state of customer experience environment, and the organization's strengths and weaknesses. These are not particularly unique to customer experience, but probably been used successfully by many of you in other programs.

First, rank each of the four principles from 0-5 in relation to the company. There are no specific guidelines attached to the rationale behind the ranking, but the numbers, especially if low and the resulting dialogue, pave the way for deeper introspection and a broader journey of discovery as the workshop develops. But, let me give you a word of warning; if done right with honesty, candour and a broad cross-section of participants, it can make for some painful and awkward moments as any serious introspection will. But you must persevere. The end results will be worthwhile and new, stronger, internal relationships will develop that will inform and guide the customer experience framework and sustain the longer term strategy.

Then use the **Stop – Start – More – Less** technique, favoured by many business and personal coaches. This requires that you take an honest and candid view of your processes, policies and other operational activities and determine which of the four actions need to be taken. This is applied to the same principles from a business, department and personal perspective and uncovers some extraordinarily valuable insights. Then the results from both exercises are linked in a grid and the resulting output identifies the most pressing needs, the most valued cultural possessions and where to start the overall process. Once again, this will turn an occasionally bright spotlight on people and processes as you discover there are no good reasons for doing certain things and nobody, especially customers, really benefit.

So to help guide us through this process, let's look at few people who are doing this well.

Zappos

While the decision to create an uncompromising customer centric culture often comes, or is influenced from the top, everyone can and should play a role in consistently delivering the company's customer service culture. In the case of Zappos, the online retailer who has taken customer experience to new levels, it wasn't just Tony Hsieh, the CEO, and his senior team; all of the employees have always had a strong voice, and are directly responsible for designing the core values on which their service culture is built. Their yearly *Culture Book* is a consistent and evolving testament to the strength and durability of this approach.

Tony Hsieh articulately and succinctly captures the upside of starting with culture in his book *Delivering Happiness*:

"At Zappos, our belief is that if you get the culture right, most of the other stuff – like great customer service, or building a long term brand or passionate employees and customers - will happen naturally on its own."

While Zappos have clearly benefitted from the effect of osmosis, I still believe it's necessary to orchestrate and blend the other three principles in equal measures to be able to create the harmony and play the music that keeps customers singing and dancing happily to your tune. Alas, many businesses forget this, and like Eric Morecambe are playing all the right notes, but not necessarily in the right order.

Four Seasons

Four Seasons is now a world famous luxury hotel brand, highly regarded for its culture of excellence. But as with many other successful businesses, it came from humble beginnings. As we learned earlier, Isadore Sharpe, the CEO and founder, launched the business with the Four Seasons

Motor Hotel in Toronto. That's right, a motel! But it wasn't the 'no tell motel'. This was a very different one, born from the principle of developing a culture where guests' comfort and the employees ability to make that happen, drove all other decisions. Growing up in Toronto in the sixties, I have fond memories of the profound changes that it drove in Canada, not just from a hotel service perspective, but in most other aspects of business and customer service.

We get an insight into his approach in the title of his book that I referenced earlier; *Four Seasons – The Story of a Business Philosophy*. As with Stephen Covey, I found Mr Sharpe's words inspirational. He provides validation and endless examples for the *Four Principles*. Throughout the book there are recurring themes of building a culture of quality and service, earning the commitment of managers and staff, creating a community of guests, employees and managers, all supported by frequent, open and honest communications. It clearly shows that this can be a business model for all companies, large and small, not just luxury hotel brands.

John Lewis

A visit to the John Lewis website sums up the importance of culture very simply and succinctly: "Our Partners will tell you that the John Lewis Partnership is a very special place to work. We believe our distinctive culture – our spirit – lies at the heart of this feeling."

It goes on to say, "The John Lewis Partnership has a visionary and successful way of doing business, putting the happiness of Partners at the centre of everything it does. It's the embodiment of an ideal, the outcome of nearly a century of endeavour to create a different sort of company, owned by Partners dedicated to serving customers with flair and fairness." If this was something that was very new, then it's possible that the sceptics among us may suggest that "It can't last." But the partnership model, and the values it embodies, was introduced in 1929 and has stood the test of many challenging times and changes in both the retail market and the wider world.

HomeServe UK

HomeServe, one of the UK's leading home assistance providers introduced their *Customer First* program in 2015. It was aimed at identifying customer situations where front line employees felt that the customer deserved a better outcome and it and it is now part of the fabric of the business. Over two thousand submissions to the program have been made, demonstrating what engaged and committed colleagues can do and allowing the front line people to really own and influence the Customer experience.

Customer First has also played a key role in implementing many of the other elements of business strategy. The submissions were categorized as either 'Good Neighbour' or 'Business Improvement'. Based on that feedback, this information guided the investment in process re-engineering and technology to reduce customer effort and make life easier for front line specialists and engineers to drive more value for customers. This also had a positive impact in reducing the cost base by eliminating unworkable policies, reducing waste and driving overall efficiencies, and yet still continues to build a strong and identifiably ethical company culture.

2. Commitment

Getting the culture right is a key cornerstone in the foundations of customer experience, but unless and until there is commitment throughout the company, it won't have the staying power or game changing influence on the company's DNA to ensure that customer experience is a living, breathing organism and not just an empty promise or a marketing slogan. As with culture, senior executive ownership, on an on-going and visibly participatory basis, is a vital element in demonstrating commitment.

Autoglass®

This leading UK consumer automotive service brand, and another company whose culture is powered by people, is a great proponent and a positive, real life example of senior management commitment.

In an article that I wrote about their customer experience vision, I highlighted the fact that when call volumes increase on cold winter mornings the whole company gets involved. Almost anyone, from the directors to the rest of the management team, take to the phones to ensure customer's calls are quickly answered and their problems solved. This not only demonstrates commitment to meeting customer needs, but also clearly shows that 'everyone is in this together' and cufflinks are no barrier to rolling sleeves up and getting down and dirty in the trenches.

Ritz Carlton

However, commitment isn't the sole responsibility of the top table and in a truly customer centric organization everyone in the company understands and demonstrates commitment in a variety of innovative and creative ways.

In his book about Ritz Carlton Hotels, *The New Gold Standard*, Joseph Michelli tells us about a general manager who endured fourteen interviews to land his role. Four were with the owners of the hotel, but ten were with other front line staff members who saw that their commitment to quality included having a voice in who joins them as colleagues. This commitment is also visibly and measurably apparent in the fact that any employee has the ability to spend up to $2000 to satisfy a customer need, without referral to a senior manager, or fear of reprisal.

Southwest Airlines

This US based, 40 year old success story, a pioneer in the low cost airline segment, has long been a poster child for great customer experience and, in particular, employee commitment. For those who haven't had the experience, the simplest way to explain it is to say that Southwest is the complete antithesis of Ryanair. The last time I flew with them I was pleasantly surprised to see the captain of the aircraft helping with check-in, and other flight crew doing whatever they could to ensure speedy yet civilized boarding and an on-time departure. As they said, "We like to think of ourselves as a Customer Service company that happens to fly airplanes (on schedule, with personality and perks along the way)." This commitment isn't accidental or occasional. As with Zappos, it is backed up by a published declaration of key commitments that supports their goal to remain a sustainable, profitable airline, and their culture of taking care of their people and the planet, while delivering a consistent and memorable customer experience.

While commitment like culture can't be mandated, it is vital that the CEO or MD leads the way and lives by the same values as the rest of the company. Four Seasons also provides a powerful and decisive example of the importance of commitment, and its impact throughout the organization. As the company grew and staff numbers increased, Isadore Sharpe recognized the importance of involving all employees in the change process, and in particular allowing them to take responsibility, and in effect self-manage. Some managers resisted this and, as Mr Sharpe believed so passionately in its alignment to the Four Seasons' culture, he decided that they needed a clear code of values, or a credo that all employees would contribute and sign up to.

As he recounted, reinforcing the credo, based on the Golden Rule of "Do unto others as you would have them do unto you", was one of the most challenging and difficult things he had to do, especially as it meant parting ways with executives who, by their lack of commitment, contradicted this policy and negatively affected the company's credibility. He was clearly proven right and said that "Enshrining the

Golden Rule as our primary working guide was the most fundamental decision in shaping our future."

This view is expressed in a similar vein by Stephen Covey who pointedly said "No involvement, no commitment" and goes on "Many organizations have people whose goals are totally different from the goals of the enterprise with reward systems that are completely out of alignment with stated value systems." Another way to look at this is to see if business leaders are committed to having customer experience metrics that determine how everyone in the organization is measured and paid, as American Express has done.

American Express

Jim Bush, President Global Network at American Express, has put this principle into practice very effectively and measurably. His team of customer service people, known as customer care professionals, are part of a measurement system that surveys the customer and gets the feedback for every servicing transaction which is used that measure their performance, complemented by some productivity indicators. Those two measures drive incentives that are the basis for compensation for the customer care professionals, and indeed all of the management team. This has not only led to increasingly happy customers, but has also contributed handsomely to the bottom line at American Express.

As with culture, commitment may be seen through different lenses and be demonstrated uniquely in each company. However, as the examples show, if it is based on a deeply shared and socialized value system, is aligned to the overall business culture and based on correct principles, then commitment, authenticity and unity will flow through your company like a welcome summer breeze.

3.   Community

The digital age and social media have brought new meanings to the concept of community. As well as being a founding principle of the declaration of customer experience, a sense of community has been around since the beginning of time. The unchanging and most enduring quality of community is, as Paul Hawken says in his book *Blessed Unrest*, that "Community resides in its ideas, not in force."

In customer experience terms, community resides comfortably and symbiotically with the other three principles. It is dependent on intertwining and bringing together the different parts of an organization to agree common goals, and ways of achieving them, in a spirit of cooperation and collaboration. When a business is successful in creating this internal spirit of community, then extending it to customers, partners and the wider geographic community just feels like a natural and rewarding thing to do.

Waitrose (John Lewis Partnership)

When you look at almost any UK customer satisfaction survey, you can always expect to see John Lewis and Waitrose high on the list. John Lewis is not only highly regarded reputationally, but is also highly profitable and the clue to why they are so successful is in the name "The John Lewis Partnership." John Spedan Lewis, the founder's son, introduced the first profit-sharing scheme in 1920 along with a representative staff council. These 'radical ideas' were based on seven basic principles which are still the driving force behind the company today and are prominently featured on the company's website. Their definition of community is that "The Partnership aims to obey the spirit as well as the letter of the law and to contribute to the wellbeing of the communities where it operates." What part of this wouldn't appeal to any right thinking and ambitious organization?

Sadly most businesses fail to even come close to this due to their overdependence on misguided and clumsily applied 'policies and procedures', or ingrained resistance to change that hampers many of their managers and other employees.

Ace Hardware

Shep Hyken, in his book *Amaze Every Customer*, features Ace Hardware as a great example of an extremely successful, but perhaps little known company whose community spirit is legendary. This has made it stand out against many of its larger, perhaps better known DIY rivals in the US such as Lowes and Home Depot, and outpaces them in terms of revenue, reputation and employee growth. While primarily a US organization, they also have operations in much of Latin America and Asia, and wherever they go they make a profound and lasting impact on the community.

In the USA since 1991, the Ace Foundation has raised over $54 million to help sick and injured kids.

The Ace store owner is totally focused on clearly identifying and standing out within their customer community, and being helpful for each and every person in that community. Their reward for this commitment is being ranked highest in customer satisfaction among home improvement retailers for a sixth consecutive year in the *JD Power and Associates* survey.

There is also an encouraging and welcome communal trend in the UK. A recent study by data analyst Kantar showed that despite the challenges faced by local shops, the larger supermarkets were losing market share to them. James Lowman, of the Association of Convenience Stores put it: "Competing with the big boys is tough, but good independents can survive and thrive by finding a point of difference – often greater customer service and a much deeper knowledge of the community."

The idea of community has limitless possibilities in terms of geography, participation and focus, but the power and reach of community in terms of its impact on customer experience is something that any business can and must aspire to, as a platform for growth, a forum for reasoned discussion and a contributor to the greater cause of the common good that a business, and its employees, can bring to life.

4.   Communication

"What we have here is a failure to communicate"

One of my favourite films is *Cool Hand Luke* starring Paul Newman and the phrase "What we've got here is (a) failure to communicate" which is spoken at different points in the movie, first by Strother Martin (as the Captain, a prison warden) and later by Paul Newman himself, (as Luke, a young prisoner).

This phrase came up from the depths of my memory when I was myself imprisoned recently. Not something we like to admit to others, but unfortunately I was held captive, in my own home, by one of the UK's largest delivery companies whilst awaiting delivery of an urgent package. The sender had requested that the item be signed for in person, 'on the threshold' thus eliminating any opportunity to have it left with a neighbour or hidden from plain sight. Unfortunately for me, not only did they not deliver as promised, but there was no communication from them to provide a reason, offer an apology and a rescheduled date and time. I had to call them to get an answer! As I later found out, the delivery driver had an accident and naturally this put the whole schedule in jeopardy. While we can empathise with the situation, the fact remains that the company was aware of the potential delay to customer deliveries and needed to both advise people and provide a replacement van.

Up to now I've celebrated companies that get things right, and as many of my posts and articles focus on the Four

Cs: I couldn't have asked for a better or more painful example of what can happen when you get things wrong. In the delivery company scenario, there were clearly problems in the underlying culture or procedures that left me in the dark. But there was also a lack of commitment from above and below and the potential for community support, i.e. another driver picking up the reins. This organization failed abysmally in almost every element of communication. In fact they didn't just violate the principle, they beat it up and left it for dead.

This lack of communication is why many businesses are failing so spectacularly and the recent BA, UA and Ryanair catastrophes mentioned previously are prime examples of this. These often self-inflicted operational failures are usually accompanied by news stories featuring angry passengers complaining of "There being nobody to let us know what was going on." Proactivity is the key to successful communication and even if there is no news, it's vital to let people know that at least somebody is aware of the issue and is seeking a resolution. In order to keep customers happy, it helps if your people are able to respond in a powerful and immediate way to service failures — using their own initiative, without waiting for a manager's okay.

The main reason for a lack of communication is the fear of litigation

It's possible though that people are not really in the position to use their initiative, or are prevented from doing so. When you look at some of the worst recent incidents such as those I've mentioned above, you have to assume that the people on the ground are afraid to say too much, or anything at all, in case it may be used against them for compensation or litigation. How else can you explain the shocking lack of information when problems strike? This may seem pretty obvious, and hardly a concept that makes the earth move. Unless you are a UK train operator, who collectively seem unable to communicate effectively with passengers, when there are problems, ("Too much sun" or the "Wrong type of snow"), that only seems to inhabit the railway world. But communicating with passengers, customers or guests is very much dependent on a company having an open and honest communication policy that builds trust, and provides reinforcement for employees to act with integrity and compassion in those critical moments of truth that can define a great customer experience.

Companies like Four Seasons, Zappos and John Lewis all feature regular two-way feedback sessions, employee briefings and councils, that give all employees and managers a voice in any decisions or issues that positively affect the quality of customer care. When employees have been involved in defining and developing the culture and committing to its delivery, having them act in harmony with the values and principles they helped create and communicate is almost second nature.

In each Four Seasons hotel there is a centrally located hotline that allows front line staff to immediately communicate any customer problems as they arise. In one case a doorman advised that a guest was unhappy that he had to wait 20 minutes for his car to be brought to him. When he heard about it, the General Manager of the hotel immediately called the guest at his office to apologize. His frankness and genuine concern did much to restore the guest's trust and faith in the hotel.

Each year the Zappos Culture Book is updated and the core values revisited as life and people change. It's actively and enthusiastically reinvigorated by all employees who share their ideals with their broader audience of customers, friends, partners and suppliers.

How the best companies manage communications

At John Lewis, power in the partnership is shared between three governing authorities: the Partnership Council, the Partnership Board and the Chairman. This ensures that communication is open, frequent, visible and truly participatory throughout the business.

The annual Southwest Airlines One Report™ measures and reports their results on their financial, social and environmental performance. This is communicated via their website and current and past years can be viewed, downloaded and compared. This isn't just a static pdf file, but increases and enhances Southwest's communication ethic by allowing anyone to customize the report to their own particular areas of interest.

Once again, I'll turn to Stephen Covey to describe the theme that runs through the communication principle of successful and caring companies. He says "Seek first to understand and then to be understood." Most companies are so busy with the second part, which is certainly important, that they neglect or pay lip service to the first.

George Bernard Shaw summed it up nicely: "The single biggest problem with communication is the illusion that it has taken place."

Unless, and until you understand what your customers truly want and need and then what they value, it will be difficult, if not impossible to get this principle working properly and to be able to communicate in a language and a way that they will understand and respond to.

But how do we know or measure what they want?

10. How do we know we're getting it right? – Measuring what Matters to Customers

"It's really hard to design products by focus groups. A lot of times, people don't know what they want until you show it to them" - Steve Jobs

In 1927 two men, separated by an ocean, but united in desire and ambition, set records in their respective sports that have stood as enduring standards of true talent and immeasurable value to their team. Baseball legend Babe Ruth hit 60 home runs for the New York Yankees, a record that stood for 34 years until Roger Maris, also of the Yankees, hit 61. Later that year Dixie Dean began a season for Everton in the old First Division of English Football and ended up scoring 60 goals, a record that has never been beaten, nor equalled. Goals, home runs and baskets tend to generate the most sports headlines, and they have generally been the currency to measure both individual and team success and to drive idolatry. However, these are frequently overrated in terms of the overall impact on a team, especially if other issues such as a leaky defence, frequent injuries or underperforming supporting players are taken into consideration.

This has parallels in business where similarly spectacular headlines and over-hyped metrics, such as stock price, total sales, and numbers of customers, have historically been used as the key indicators to rate success. For many businesses and investors, these have been found to be less dependable, dangerously unstable and unpredictable over the longer term. We only have to look at the banking or utilities industries in the UK and more recently, share price roller coasters such as BT and Centrica, for evidence of that. While the big numbers can still resonate, more attention is being focused on data that delivers the most relevant and timely insights – the combination of data sets that enable effective and intelligent investment - that go into achieving success, whether that's on the field, in the standings, at the box office or the board room.

The Best Figure - Where Contribution and Value Meet

When Babe Ruth earned $80,000 in 1930 a reporter asked him why he had made more money than the President, Herbert Hoover, Ruth famously answered, "I had a better year". In a statistics driven game this was an early example of having the right insight or data to back-up his claim and measure his success, however glibly it was stated.

Back in England, where scoring was reputationally valued but financially less rewarding, Dixie Dean's weekly wage topped out at £8, (yes really!) and it was many years before footballers in England were paid a living wage. Dixie once remarked to George Best when discussing players' salaries, "When I was playing, I couldn't afford a pair of boots never mind boutiques." Now it's off the scale in the other direction and has no relationship to actual sporting talent, organizational intelligence or value to the team. Value is measured more in shirt sales and other spurious commercial links such as Newcastle United's sponsorship by pay day loans company, Wonga. This led Nick Forbes, the leader of

Newcastle city council, to say he was "Appalled and sickened" that Newcastle would "sign a deal with a legal loan shark".

Computer says "yes" and "no"

Let's return to North America, where in the past few years there has been some game changing (literally) activity in the sporting financial landscape. Although there is still some silly money being thrown around, the concept of salary caps and greater financial prudence is beginning to gain currency and acceptance, although probably out of necessity rather than increased common sense or discovery of a social conscience. This has led to a slow, subtle, but seemingly irreversible change in how sports teams rate, evaluate, and ultimately sign and pay for players.

Major League Baseball is where this change has been most keenly felt and where statistics have generated legions of anoraks for many years. The catalyst for this change actually started in the late 70's when Bill James, who had no experience as a writer, but had a huge obsession with baseball, started collecting his own brand of statistics and began publishing his *Baseball Abstract*. What made his approach radically different, was that he took serious issue with many of the statistics that had been historically used to rate players and teams and to demonstrate and value success. It took some time before James's statistics had a measurable effect on the game, and many people, both inside and outside baseball, thought of him as an eccentric and misguided journalist or just a bored number cruncher.

That was until Billy Beane became the general manager of the Oakland A's in 1997. The best-selling author Michael Lewis tells the story of Billy, the Oakland As, and his discovery of James' statistical approach, in his excellent book *Moneyball*. He hits an early and resounding home run in the book when he states that Bill James found that "The statistics were not merely inadequate: they lied. And the lies they told led the people that ran baseball to misjudge their players and mismanage their games."

An intelligent approach to the price of success

The book's main theme is charting the success of the Oakland A's and Billy Beane's role in it. The A's, who, as a smaller market club, similar perhaps to Bournemouth or Watford in the EPL, simply didn't have the resources of the bigger teams such as the New York Yankees or Boston Red Sox to attract the top stars and newly minted and often overrated prospects. He tells how Billy Beane used a whole new range of metrics to help the A's to sign players who not only didn't show up on other teams' radar and scouting systems, but were thought to be significantly inferior to the highly paid stars and prospects that the other teams were courting. And this wasn't just a one year phenomenon; Oakland has consistently out-performed the richer teams by staggering amounts, and, although last season was less successful, the long term financial results speak for themselves. One statistic that puts this into perspective is the amount of money each Major League Baseball team has 'paid' for a win. Based on a formula developed by Doug Pappas, a leading authority on baseball finance, over a three year period the A's paid around $500 thousand per win. Compare this with the nearly $3 million that richer teams such as the Baltimore Orioles and Texas Rangers spent, for far less success and far more player aggravation and mediocrity.

A new way of thinking – Powerful combinations lead to hidden valuation

In a nutshell Billy Beane started to rethink baseball and looked for new baseball knowledge. He used a systematic, scientific investigation of the sport to utilize data and drive insight that hadn't traditionally been used to value players. In doing this, he uncovered and mined hidden gems of players that might have otherwise been left to languish in lower leagues, or never make it, all because of the historic talent evaluation prejudices rooted in baseball traditions. He was able to start looking at players in very different ways and to use measures and evaluation, both physical and psychological, in powerful combinations that showed a players true worth and made a lasting impact on baseball history. Billy has just become a minority owner at Barnsley in the English Championship and their fans are clearly hoping that some of his magic can make the transatlantic trip along with him.

Perhaps if Man U. and other EPL teams hadn't lead with their wallet and utilized some of his ideas, they would have never signed some of the players that failed to produce as expected, or that the excessive transfer fees warranted. Recently, that old Dutch master, Louis van Gaal, the former

Man U. manager stated that some of the players that were in this category, and subsequently left, didn't fit the club's culture. Perhaps because climatically or socially (not having London's night club availability?) becoming Mancunians wasn't ever on their bucket list. Unfortunately as Louis is a throwback to the old days, similar to a lot of baseball traditionalists, he failed to grasp the fact that this is something that Man U needed to find out before they signed them. What was needed was a more detailed analysis of individual attitudes, behaviours, cultural backgrounds and other non-football specific traits. Had they done this and identified and recognized some early warning signs, then they would have also passed on a host of their other expensive failures and concentrated on real potential talent who were ready, willing and able to do the hard work, in order to succeed, as many of the Man U. "Class of 92", such as Paul Scholes, Ryan Giggs and Nicky Butt had done.

Customer experience lessons from the A's

There are significant parallels between the A's and business today, and how many companies still use outdated and irrelevant statistics to delude themselves into thinking they are delivering a great service, and that their customers love them. Realistic, forward thinking businesses are developing new approaches to customer experience by rethinking customer engagement and being smarter about what data they use to build and maintain their strategy, and how they use this insight to retain and 'sign' new customers. In the early parts of the 21st century, many businesses were as profligate as football teams and threw large sums of money at the technology companies that flashed their eyelashes at them. This resulted in the business opening their kimonos to let them install high priced CRM systems, flashy CTI solutions and other shiny new toys that, like many footballers, blew the money, garnered the headlines, but never delivered the goods.

Companies would have been better to have been a disciple of Bill James, rather than solely worshipping at the altar of Hi-tech. His overriding message in his *Abstracts* was that people like Billy Beane were on the receiving end of a false idea of what makes a successful baseball player, and that if you challenge conventional wisdom you'll find ways to do things much better than they are currently being done. This is a seemingly obvious reverse play on the definition of insanity.

Organizations that are redefining customer engagement are now implementing that advice without perhaps realizing its genesis, and are starting to reduce the inefficiency caused by sloppy data or tired, outdated metrics such as NPS or CSAT. It's not that I have anything particularly against either of these, but they both represent a single number metric and, in terms of truly and fairly valuing the experience that each customer has, both are inadequate. And in those cases where a deeper, more meaningful long term relationship is desired, it's wholly lacking in emotional or personal context. Asking a customer whether they would recommend a company to their friends or colleagues (and surely never knowing if they have) and whether they are satisfied seems mildly interesting, but far from conclusive in identifying both current company opinions and future decisive actions. And I'm not alone in this view. A recent poll conducted by *Marketforce* showed that 66% of respondents believed that a combination of metrics, especially those featuring experiential and emotional values, will be the most widely used method in the next 5 years.

Understanding the relationship between customer actions, attitudes, responses and value created will identify what actually makes a difference in customer terms and creates Positive Customer Outcomes (PCO). This is a measure based on a combination of values that I've developed and started to use with customers as an effective and enduring measure of success in individual interactions and over the longer term. As it is far more definitive in both name and value, it also reflects positively on the employee or business process as it's difficult to have a high PCO score without an equally positive employee performance. That in turn can be translated into increased sales, customer retention, employee engagement and other more qualitative metrics that actually mean something and can be measured and analysed for their effect on the overall business.

The early baseball statistics innovators realized that each event on the field had an expected run value and contributed to the overall performance of the team. This in turn showed *how* to account for a players performance by the number of runs scored. But *how much* each event on the field was worth was much harder to figure out. On drilling deeper, teams found that it contained rich seams of data that could provide the answers that had never previously been recorded, or investigated fully.

Find the real value and what counts most for customers

Similarly in business, every action has a PCO value and the statistics that you need to consider and combine will change depending on the type of business, the role of the contact centre and/or other interactions across various channels. But they're worth digging for. As an example: rather than just figuring out success based on overall sales volume or individual purchases, we should look deeper. An organization I worked with started to take a more in-depth look and went beyond the basics to ask some much more creative and illuminating questions. What is the ratio between store visits, web sessions or phone calls per £ of sales? How many customers does each customer service agent speak to for every £ of revenue? What is the average call length of successful (sale) and unsuccessful (no sale) calls? Does a customer buy more when they call early in the day or later? Does this depend on hold time, or how easy it was to get to the right place, or speak to the right person?

These may seem inconsequential, irrelevant or difficult to uncover, but in this world of excessive excitement caused by an unrealistic overdependence on often expensive Big Data, this data already exists, is available and at a low cost because you already own it or can quite easily get it.

As Billy Beane discovered, just because nobody else was interested in a certain player, didn't mean they weren't valuable. In fact for him, as time went on and his quirky selections were vindicated, this made them even more potentially valuable.

Bringing Data to Life – Turning Insight into Action

Maximizing the value of your insight may seem obvious, but it's clear from my own interactions as a customer that very little that I say or do, or how I use products or services, is ever used creatively to deliver a better experience or to achieve a strong PCO.

For whatever reason, many organizations continue to operate with beliefs and biases, many of which are long held, honestly formed, but fatally flawed and operationally Inaccurate when used to evaluate performance and determine customer needs and preferences. As the grandfather of customer experience, Heraclitus, once remarked, "The only thing that is constant is change." Billy Beane showed that by continuing to expand his statistical view, he found traits and player attributes that everyone else was overlooking. Even when it was clear that the A's were onto something, many in baseball derided it as just luck and continued to believe that baseball statistics were the pure accomplishments of men against other men, or perhaps in business parlance, one company against another. But this was wrong, and as Bill James noted, "They are accomplishments of men in combination with their circumstances". A subtle, but extremely critical difference.

But, innovative journeys into data and insight don't just benefit customers. In his recent eBook *Design Driven Feedback*, Max Israel puts it succinctly when he describes the value in combining art with science to elevate enterprise feedback management. "Over time, design-driven feedback has come to encompass not just how feedback feels from the point of view of a person asked to share it, but also the legions of employees to whom we direct it. In short, design-driven feedback is a movement dedicated to leveraging not just technology and analytical skills but also design and creative ones to make feedback deeply engaging for consumer and worker alike. It has the power to do both."

These deeper and more personal insights revive and enhance how companies use customer experience data. By 'humanizing' data, you can also inform staffing decisions, technology investments, new product introductions and in turn develop huge advances in organizational engagement. This has a waterfall effect and can cascade over many parts of the business refreshing, cleansing and bringing fresh new life to help the business grow and prosper. This is vital as customers are changing fast and conventional wisdom may have had its place in the sun.

Businesses must take a certain leap of faith and start looking in places and finding stats that don't appear to interest others, and to turn that data into insights that create rich and contextual customer experiences. Much as we hear about 'intangibles' among top athletes, there are additional layers of creativity, innovation and personalization that go beyond just connecting with customers, as there are connecting bat to ball. So don't slow down or stop swinging for the fences. As Babe Ruth said, "Never let the fear of striking out get in your way."

11. It's the Principles That Count – Things To Do Now

"In times of universal deceit, telling the truth becomes a revolutionary act"" – George Orwell

In an increasingly competitive business world, many organizations state loud and proud that customer experience is a key strategic initiative that promises great things for their customers. Published statistical evidence, from the likes of Which? Magazine and the Institute for Customer Service, aligned with my personal experiences, suggests this isn't happening with quite the stunning impact or regularity that businesses would have us believe, and demonstrates a clear disconnect between their ambition and our reality.

The clue is in the word initiative. This suggests that rather than being a true company-wide, senior management led, transformational change, it's a short term cosmetic exercise involving only a few inspired individuals who often lack the full financial support, employee involvement and executive commitment to truly make a difference. I hope that our journey through the *Four Principles* has convinced you that while instantly recognizable as important ideas in almost any human dimension, they also have a strong correlation to customer experience, and that organizational alignment is vital to bringing that strategy to life. So, let's finish this stage of the journey with some ideas and concepts that may not be new, but may certainly be due for a refresh, and that you can and should do now.

And, as Billy Beane found, maybe nobody else is doing them!

1. Look in the mirror – Put your own house in order

It's difficult to begin a journey to a new destination, including corporate transformation, unless we have a clear understanding of where we are today, and what our corporate culture represents. In other words, what is the current state of the nation? Only you can decide how deep and wide this needs to be, but there will always be strong, influential clues from customers and colleagues. It's an excellent opportunity to take an operational review and also a philosophical view, examining your raison d'être. This could come under the heading of your purpose, your mission and why you are in business. And the answer to the last one isn't simply 'to make a profit'. Well, not for everybody.

While many companies use Voice of the Customer information (VOC), or Net Promoter Scores (NPS) to see how others see them, real analysis and authenticity go way beyond that. Both VOC and NPS are, for many, important measures and high level, key indicators of how a business is doing, just as a thermometer is for our personal health.

However, getting immersed in the customer service at a human level, and that means both sides of the interaction, will often provide more accurate feedback than looking at surveys. Because unless you take an outside-in-view and involve people from across the business in a deeper, more introspective and comprehensive view of the company, you won't be truly able to see yourselves as others see you. This doesn't necessarily involve huge numbers of people or a massive expense, just a willingness to invest in a better future. My own experience has shown that a small employee team given accessibility, responsibility and accountability will relish the opportunity to make a difference, and a press gang approach won't be necessary. So, start advertising for volunteers now. For further insight I'd suggest reading *Delivering Happiness*, Tony Hsieh's book about how they did it at **Zappos**.

Once you have the team in place and they realize it's not just a vanity exercise, it won't be hard to get them to share their own experiences. They'll tell you where the bodies are buried, probably produce a detailed map and share what words they have to say to customers, policies they have to enforce or actions they take, that embarrasses them and that they would change. While these won't be the only people to provide feedback and get the show on the road, theirs will be honest, clear and free of corporate double talk.

2. Visualize the destination – Plan the Journey

Anyone with young children, or an impatient partner will have heard that immortal phrase "Are we there yet?" during a long journey. Customer experience is no different. Once the journey starts everyone will want to get there yesterday, but until the Star Trek transporter becomes a reality, patience will be required. However, very much like a holiday trip, it doesn't mean that the journey itself can't be made more enjoyable, educational and incrementally valuable to all participants.

Once the initial small team is together, you need to plan the journey with realistic, achievable milestones. It's vital to have frequent stopovers at appropriate points on a customer experience map that draws frequently on the *Four Principles* for guidance, location and direction. Use these to evaluate your current performance through your customer's eyes. Use your own operational realities, and internal road-blocks, to define where you are on the journey, how you're doing, how far you have to go and what, if any, detours you may have to make. While making these detours is quite natural, probably necessary, and known in agile vernacular as 'fail fast' , it's critical that you have the right map in your hands for your stated destination. Because even the most detailed and comprehensive map of France probably won't get you to Cornwall.

3. Tell them why you care – Values to live by

The various companies that we visited earlier- **John Lewis, Zappos, Four Seasons, HomeServe** and **Metro Bank** - are leaders in customer experience and business success. They have all based their culture of excellence on a strong set of core values, or a code of behaviour that has real purpose and meaning and isn't a hastily devised, slick slogan from an advertising intern. This is not mandated solely from above, but is based on shared beliefs, values, and practices. This is one of the key outputs from increased employee involvement where all of the employees have a strong voice, and are directly responsible for developing the fundamentals on which their service culture is built.

Publishing these prominently on websites, in-store and supporting them authentically through regular communications for all to see, mean that they are constantly tested, evaluated and validated by customers, and improved by staff, as evidenced by Zappos' yearly *Culture Book*. This creates an uncompromising customer centric culture that is everyone's responsibility and where there is a direct correlation between living up to these standards every time, with every customer, and promotes employee/company growth. While a business may not need the ten core values that **Zappos** have, or be as detailed as The John Lewis Partnership Constitution, these statements contain values and ideas that large and small businesses can use effectively as both a benchmark and a signpost on their customer experience strategy journey. Borrowing and/or adopting a few of these values and ideas would be a great start and likely to be favourably received throughout the organizations.

4. Show them how you care – Walking the walk

Customers are becoming harder to fool. I suspect they always were, PT Barnum notwithstanding. Consequently they'll see through fluffy, unsupported, 'mission statements', unfulfilled commitments and meaningless tag lines, developed in a flash of marketing brilliance.

Metro Bank, the UK's newest High Street entry, has been busy "Creating a culture of Yes", that includes no stupid bank rules, unlimited dog biscuits, free pens and free coin counting machines and a well-regarded canine mascot, Sir Duffield II. While this may seem to some as a little fluffy (that's a description of the ideas, not the dog), they reflect the fact that great customer experience can and should be enjoyable. Especially when the founding principles are based on common sense. This is a living and visible embodiment of their commitment to a different banking experience and is on everyday display, regardless of which store you go to. Are these things hugely different from the other banks and therefore likely to significantly enhance your experience? Well, definitely yes, and positively, because they are highly visible, emotionally connecting and entertaining symbols of an organization that is delightfully different and totally committed to a culture that matches the model and reflects their purpose in business.

5. Follow the Leader – Commitment still starts at the top

Commitment isn't the sole responsibility of the senior leadership, but without gaining that in the early stages of strategy development, it will be difficult to maintain the momentum and transformational change required. As we saw earlier Isadore Sharp recounted in his book, *Four Seasons –The Story of a Business Philosophy* that a lack of commitment from his senior managers, to his idea of increased employee responsibility, resulted in some difficult personnel decisions. This ultimately ended positively with the development of their credo that is still the standard, and that shapes and guides employee behaviour and customer service. While the credo was not mandated solely by him, without his relatively gentle but persuasive influence, the company may not have developed into the legendary customer service organization they are so well known for today.

Leaders like Isadore Sharpe and Tony Hsieh who, along with his employees at **Zappos**, have been equally instrumental in the creation of core values that stick, both recognize that this can't be simply delegated, and that senior executive ownership, on an on-going and visibly participatory basis, is a vital element in mobilizing, demonstrating and maintaining commitment.

6. Invite others on the journey – It's a community effort

We saw earlier that in the initial stages of customer experience strategy development, it may be a small focused team with committed, senior level support that leads the charge. However, widening the scope and influence and increasing the value of co-creation by involving customers, employees and other senior managers is another important stage in the strategy. One of the most common and deceptively simple ways that many organizations achieve this, is to have employees shadow a colleague in a different role or department for a day. This, more than anything, will let your colleague walk in your shoes, see the world through different eyes and be more understanding of the challenges that you face, while potentially seeing ways of changing and improving processes that you might overlook. Forest – Trees!

Once you've started this engine it may be hard to stop, or slow down. But that's a good thing, and will provide employees with a far stronger understanding of different parts of the business, the challenges that their colleagues may face and how they can collaborate more effectively to resolve customer issues before they go viral. One of the other benefits of this is to develop more well-rounded employees who can step into the breach when needed, and gain valuable new skills that can make their career more interesting and lead to more responsible and financially rewarding roles.

7. Taking it to the streets – Sharing with those who matter

Community spirit and well-being also extend beyond the enterprise and have limitless possibilities, and endless benefits for all parties when they are seen as truly and believably altruistic. We saw this earlier with **ACE Hardware**, who through the ACE Foundation, play a key role in giving back to those less fortunate.

Companies such as **Autoglass®** in the UK are a great example of the power of community, and they have long been active and involved members of the local and wider community, where engaged and like-minded employees demonstrate their willingness to help others less fortunate than themselves. The company has regularly provided its contact centre facilities and volunteers for *Children in Need* and *Comic Relief* donation lines, as well as putting on employee sponsored events supporting a number of local charities.

HomeServe already supports more vulnerable members of the community by identifying any potential social and existential issues, and helping them in their homes on a daily basis, as part of their normal service. They've also helped the less fortunate by having their plumbing apprentices, currently completing their training at Walsall College, give something back to the community by volunteering to feed homeless people in Birmingham city centre.

Whether you can offer a whole contact centre, one person to answer a phone, or deliver meals and comfort to the vulnerable, companies that give back to the community, especially through the participation of employees, generally end up with a far stronger sense of purpose beyond simply making a profit. So get involved, because no matter how small it might seem to your business or your people, it'll mean the world to somebody.

8. Spread the word – Communicate early, often and honestly

In a world that seems permanently embroiled in strife and filled with horror stories, spreading good news may not be popular with the BBC or the tabloids, but as humans we relish and appreciate every last morsel of life-affirming communication. If we look at some of the more recent and public customer service issues that have hit the headlines, the ones that evaporate the quickest are those that are accompanied by a reasoned and honest response from the company in question. Those companies that recover the situation in a compassionate and responsible way generally end up in positive territory or, at minimum, significantly limiting the damage.

As a case in point, **Tesco** was inundated with negative social media posts about the poor conditions of one of its stores near London. Rather than hide behind corporate doublespeak, then **Tesco** chairmen Sir Richard Broadbent, in a Sunday Times article a few days later, commented that when he arrived he found a company that had "Lost touch with the outside world". He added, "we don't defend problems, we tackle them." He finished by saying that, "The company that provides the best relationship with the customer will win — not through product, but through the best experience." It appears that his message is getting through and some positive changes have taken place at the store in question.

While the **Tesco** recovery may still take some time, and they clearly have wider business challenges, compare that with what happens when snow, or the wrong kind of sun, rain or leaves, cause disruption at UK Airports and with train operators. Honesty has never been their best policy! Most people understand that weather issues can cause delays and cancellations. But what drives most of us crazy, is that these companies seem totally incapable of providing meaningful, accurate and timely information that can keep stranded passengers updated and aware of how long they'll be delayed, provide alternate travel options and similar guidance. So no matter how painful it may seem in the short term, get the word out. Bad news early has remarkably forgiving and recuperative benefits over time.

9. The communication network – Is everyone plugged in?

Thomas Fuller said, "Charity begins at home, but should not end there." The same is very true of communication. When you first start on your customer experience journey, the communication network may not be as universal or as a finely developed as you may wish, but creating a foundation and mechanism for dialogue, both internally and externally, is critical to the long term success of your strategy. Companies like **Four Seasons, Zappos, John Lewis** and **Southwest Airlines and HomeServe** all feature regular two-way feedback sessions, employee briefings and customer councils, that give all employees and managers a voice in any decisions, or issues that positively affect the quality of customer care. When employees have been involved in defining and developing the culture and committing to its delivery, having them act in harmony with the values and principles they helped create and communicate, becomes second nature and nobody has to tell them what to do.

So don't assume that everyone in the organization is tuned into information about the customer experience strategy, either formally or informally. Establish a regular and flexible communication network that ensures regular updates and good news stories, and that makes the headlines for all the right reasons!

10. Do it Now – You Company Needs You!

I've lost count of the number of organizations that told me that "The time wasn't right to invest in CX". The very real nature of a constantly changing business landscape, whether that's driven by innovation (Uber, Airbnb), politics (Brexit, Trump), Technology (Digital, AI), Employees (Millennials, Gen Z, Geezers) means that all of this customer experience stuff needs to be continually reviewed, refined and reenergized. As with many things in life, delay or procrastination is rarely a sustainable strategy. While it's clearly beneficial to have the whole organization on board, and especially the senior management, sometimes they'll need convincing and you'll have to show them some early, but recognizable progress. This is where the concept of incremental gains, made famous by the Sky cycling team, can play a big part. You may need to start by fixing the obviously broken pieces, or start with one issue in one department, and this may be an excellent way to focus attention on the overall task at hand. Demonstrate measurable results. This focus on a small element, but one with significant returns, will help develop a following, and more people will want to join in.

Regardless of your role or position in the company, you really can make a difference. Start by suggesting a Proof of Concept (POC) that will focus on an operational or procedural change that doesn't entail any vast expenditure, or resources and can create a new experience for customers, or dramatically change an existing one. This may be in one small part of the company with the highest number of complaints, or where extraordinary costs are being occurred. A key element of this will be to get immediate customer feedback and to make it clear that you are conducting this exercise to address specific issues. Being authentic, honest and showing that you really care about their problems will do much to increase the company's value in their eyes and provide valuable feedback that can be shared across the business.

In any customer experience program, the one thing that is a constant is the customer. Their expectations may change in terms of time, money, ease etc., but they still want one thing, whether it's business, a story, a movie and more importantly, in their life.

They want a happy and (winning) ending!

FINAL THOUGHTS

In his introduction to his book *The Great Acceleration*, Robert Colville asks an important question. "What single quality best defines how our society is changing? Is it that life is getting fairer, or more equal, or more prosperous? No, it is that life is getting faster."

This is a question that could well be asked about customer experience, especially in terms of progress for fairness and equality towards customers and employees. Many businesses are struggling to keep up with the pace of change in their customer's expectations, and it feels as if many have given up trying, or just don't care.

In the relatively brief time that it has taken me to complete this book, there have been many more examples of how customers are being failed abysmally by companies in all industries. Airlines, train companies and banks are once again leading the way in the race to the bottom, and it's not all accidental, born of organizational impotency, corporate cowardice or executive incompetence. Andrew Elison writing in *The Times* to comment on a new study, called *Concentration, not Competition: the State of UK Consumer Markets*, and it doesn't pull any punches.

"The sad reality is most big businesses treat customers with contempt. They take every chance to rip them off. Telecoms companies hard-sell vulnerable pensioners upgrades they don't need, banks exploit financial ignorance, energy companies overcharge knowing we will not switch as others are just as bad."

He goes on to say.

"The Social Market Foundation report identifies the problem — many markets are just not competitive enough. Companies do not fear losing us. They have grown flabby and lazy on the profits of comfortable positions and we all suffer as a result."

There is additional supporting evidence for the lack of corporate actions and moral responsibility from Jill Insley, The Sunday Times Consumer Champion. In a year end article entitled *"Half a million reasons to write to Jill Insley"* she reflects on the amount of compensation she recovered for readers in 2017, and the reasons behind the initial problems for her readers. She says that "They have usually fallen victim to poor customer service, shoddy products, out-of-date computer systems, under-trained staff, badly written documentation, poorly explained processes."

Clearly there's no shortage of frustration and cynicism and as we saw with Dave Carroll and United Airlines, the digital explosion and easy access to social media has shaken the customer from their slumbers. Companies recognize the damage that can now be done by one disgruntled customer and while not changing willingly, are slowly getting the message. However, they have some catching up to do as the companies that started out by putting the customer first have this caring and customer winning attitude as part of their DNA, and that is a serious building block to have to replicate.

History is on our side – Companies that care first also last longest

A visionary such as Isadore Sharp at **Four Seasons**, who started with the end in mind and has continued to fly the flag equally strongly and proudly for his employees as well as customers. Tony Hsieh at Zappos, while occasionally courting controversy with innovative employee management schemes, has done much to further the cause of great customer service and strong, consistent employee engagement. Paula Nickolds and her predecessors at **John Lewis** enthusiastically, proudly and respectfully wear the mantle and carry on the traditions established by John Spedan Lewis almost a century ago. Greg Reed, stands tall with his thoughtful, inclusive and innovative leadership that led an inspiring turnaround at **HomeServe**. Also **LL Bean** would be proud of the legacy of great customer centric service that is still being delivered in his eponymous retail operation, and that continues to be financially and reputationally successful more than 100 years after selling its first pair of waterproof hunting and fishing boots.

Even in the monumentally arrogant, indisputably indifferent and seemingly terminally crooked world of banking, there are small but significant signs of human beings at the helm. In the UK, **Metro Bank, Tandem** and **Atom**, while perhaps still niche players, are growing in market share and offer hope for the future. Their founders truly want to show us that they are out to quench the financial firestorm that threatens to engulf the industry, and they are not the same bunch of pyrotechnic despots epitomized by Fred the Shred, Bob the 'Diamond Geezer' and, more recently, John Stumpf of **Wells Fargo**.

So is this a revolution or an evolution? I'm not sure it really matters as long as there is a change. If it is revolution, I'd like to see it include a 'consensual' arrangement between all key stakeholders, which I guess in itself is revolutionary. We need to find new and collaborative ways for customers and businesses to work cooperatively for the common good. Hopefully this concept isn't too socialist for our American friends, especially those who have been held-up and betrayed by the likes of Wells Fargo, Enron and other corporate bandits.

This is where one or more customers, the New Consumer that I introduced earlier, would play a leading, on-going and strategically and operationally binding role. Having customers and employees represented on boards is a good first step, but they also need to be in the engine room. Have them join staff on the shop floor, the contact centre, on the delivery van, anywhere that customers congregate. On the digital front, have them engage in design sessions with the IT team who create those wonderfully artistic but operational bereft websites that we all "404" out of every day, and Apps that really don't do anything of value for customers. How about if they spoke to end users face-to-face and understood their expectations on how to interact with devices, applications, and systems in the real world?

Get real people involved operationally as well as strategically. Let them sit in on employee interviews, CX strategy sessions, marketing campaign planning, in fact any activity where their real world input can lead to mutually beneficial and longer lasting business success.

There's no one size fits all for this and this is meant to be the opening salvo, not the Full Monty, but hopefully you get the general idea. The Gettysburg address was short on words (272) but long on intentions, actions and sustainability. The Romans will tell you, it'll take more than 24 hours, but unless you really do get customers more involved *in* your business, they'll get less involved *with* your business – financially.

It's clear that across the globe from a political perspective, populism is not just an occasional irritant. It's becoming an earthquake of serious seismic proportions. Irrespective of our individual views of Brexit, Trumpism, and the various nationalistic movements, things are changing fast. Businesses, as well as people, must recognize this, and, with a nod to an earlier comment, while change isn't mandatory, neither is survival. This will not only depend on just keeping up, but being one of the leaders.

Translating populism into positive and measurable action requires a more collaborative, engaging and caring environment. While that may be a pipe dream in many nationalistic and existential struggles, it's not beyond the realms of possibility in a corporate world. All of us, as customers, continue to have multiple daily interactions that shape our view of what a great customer experience should be. And this is slowly yet surely having a positive impact on businesses where we work. It is creating a culture of increased responsibility, enhanced engagement and new levels of employee empowerment that is clearly more than the sum of its influences.

Many businesses now understand that anyone in the organization, not just the senior managers, can have ideas that can change the company for the better. While I realize that encouraging ideas, stimulating innovation and employee 'suggestion boxes' are not brand new, ensuring that employee voices are heard and used to drive change in a business is gaining more currency. The front line, customer-facing teams, along with customers, will have totally different experiences; see things from broader perspectives and generate better, more relevant ideas than someone focused entirely on finance, operations or HR.

This isn't necessarily new either, especially among the brands that I've highlighted throughout the book. But, it is being celebrated and socialized more than ever and I had an opportunity to see this in action as a judge in the European Customer Service Awards. I was fortunate to observe some very innovative and creative presentations that clearly demonstrated that change is happening, and that cross-functional collaboration was a key driver. In particular, I saw frequent and powerful examples of motivated people forming communities around a meaningful and common purpose. One of the central themes was "Your ideas aren't just appreciated. They're necessary and vital to delivering successful customer experience."

Seeing this strong evidence of change up close and personal had a profound effect on me. The presentations featured a diversity of cross-business roles, a true democratization of ideas, and hard operational, reputational and financial evidence of corporate success and personal fulfilment.

So the revolution is upon us and while I realize that their forces haven't yet stormed the barricades of every boardroom, the coaches are booked, the beer loaded and they're on their way. The new consumers are increasingly more discerning, vocal and active and my judging experience showed Senior Executives, with strong support from their customer teams are starting to realize that when customers win, their hearts and minds will surely follow!

APPENDIX

Customer Stories

While I've included brief example of how various companies have deployed their customer experience strategy, I also felt it was worth spending a little more time with those businesses that really do have CX working for them.

1. *Home Serve*

2. *Autoglass®*

3. *Metro Bank*

The HomeServe Recovery

Margaret McDonald couldn't stop shaking and shivering as the temperature in her small terraced house continued to drop precipitously. It gets cold and dark early on a windswept December night in Glasgow, and 2011 was a particularly cold winter. With her boiler not working, the cold bit ever deeper into her old bones and she started to see her breath in the cold night air.

It wasn't as if Margaret was a stranger to hardship, privation and tough times. During World War II she had worked at the munitions factory in Bishopton and, after the war, living in the Gorbals, she'd felt the ongoing, relentless pain of poverty that many others in the area shared. But with the resolution and determination that Scots are known for, she and her husband David, who worked in the shipyards on the Clyde, were able to move to a small, neat and well-kept Southside house where they lived for over 50 years.

David had died five years earlier, and while Margaret was still strong willed, proud and stoic, even she realized that at 92, she needed to find help to fix her boiler, and fast. Then she remembered that she had signed up for boiler service plan, but couldn't remember who it was with. She anxiously, but carefully, went through the drawer in the living room where she kept her important papers but couldn't find anything. Then she had a thought and opened the door to the small cupboard that housed the boiler and there on the shelf was an envelope. She looked inside and sure enough there was an official looking document from a company called HomeServe. "Yes" she cried, this was it, the service policy. She searched the document for a phone number and when she found it, dialled the number with a sense of relief and hope that help might soon be on the way.

After struggling through a number of choices from the automatic answering service, a welcoming human voice answered the phone. As Mrs MacDonald voice expressed concern and worry, the adviser patiently and empathetically walked her through the process. But then her hopes were shattered;

"I'm sorry Mrs MacDonald but this policy expired a month ago," said the adviser.

"What can I do," she said," I'm really cold and can't really stand another night without heat."

The adviser replied, "I can re-start your policy and we can see when we can get an engineer to come out. It will be £150. Can you give me a credit card to process the payment?"

Unfortunately she couldn't as she always paid for everything by cheque or cash; she'd never really trusted credit or debit cards.

The adviser said, "I'm sorry, the only thing I can do is to send you out a renewal form and you can send a cheque with the payment."

Now Mrs Macdonald began to panic. "Can't you send somebody? I'll give them the cheque." The adviser knew the answer, even though it chilled her to the core to deliver it.

"I'm sorry, we're not able to dispatch an engineer if the policy has lapsed." This was all part of the focus on sales and increasing shareholder value that underpinned the HomeServe management's marketing strategy at that time. Delivering service to someone who hadn't paid definitely didn't fit that model! This wasn't the first time that the adviser, Gemma Hammond, had encountered this type of call, and it always seemed as if it was an elderly or otherwise vulnerable customer to whom she had to deliver the bad news. But she knew it was more than her job was worth to go against company policy. She made a note of Mrs MacDonald's name and added it to her growing list of similar calls she had taken, and once again made a silent vow that one day she'd be able to really help Mrs MacDonald and others like her. Little did she know that the cavalry was already mounting up and help was on the way.

The chickens come home to roost and the bill is £30 Million

Regulatory bodies take their fair, and sometimes deserved, share of flack, but in the wake of the financial crisis of 2008/9, a new sense of responsibility became evident and many began to look for where the bodies were buried. In particular the Financial Services Authority, now the Financial Conduct Authority FCA), realized that the mis-selling of financial service products, in particular Payment Protection Insurance (PPI), was a huge issue and all of the major banks had to make provisions for the vast fines. They weren't the only ones and while the FCA was trawling for the bigger fish, they also hooked a smaller, but seriously misbehaving organization in the insurance sector. Yes, it was HomeServe.

The full FSA Report lays out in excruciating detail the list of transgressions attributed to HomeServe and it made for difficult reading for people like Gemma who really cared for customers and wanted to treat them fairly and compassionately. Tracey McDermott, the FCA's director of enforcement and financial crime, sums it up with this comment.

"This is a serious case, one that has warranted our largest retail conduct fine [of £30 million] and generated a sizeable bill [£17 million] for consumer redress. HomeServe is another example of a firm that has acted without proper regard for its customers over a long period of time. HomeServe promises to provide customers with peace of mind when things go wrong. In fact the firm's culture, controls and remuneration structures meant that staff was focussed on quantity not quality and there were customers that paid the price for that."

The report went on to say "That the FCA considers that the failings were particularly serious given that a significant proportion of its customers were of retirement age and therefore more vulnerable. HomeServe has been contacting potentially affected customers to provide redress where appropriate. This customer contact exercise is on-going."

The last two sentences could have been plucked from a PR guidebook, or penned by a marketing whiz to convince the world that these financial services footpads and miscreants had found redemption and truly mended their ways. But the banks, in true three wise monkey fashion, seemed to be taking a long time to learn their lessons. While they all had their knuckles rapped, we regularly find them in our pockets extracting excessive fees and charges to the extent that two years ago Which? Magazine launched a petition to get them to address the issue. However, HomeServe's People are cut from different cloth and their action plan was based on authenticity and commitment that formed the foundation and guiding principles of the new culture that evolved. After the appropriate "mea culpas", they set their sights not just on redemption, but rebirth, and no one was happier, or more willing to be the Midwife, than Gemma Hammond.

Fixing the Leaks - Finding their Way

As both a serial complainer as a customer, and a customer experience practitioner, I've felt particular appreciative of the Germans for giving us the word *schadenfreude*. With no shortage of companies constantly and consistently ripping off customers with apparent impunity, when that day of reckoning arrives, I'm as happy as anyone to see a transgressor get their comeuppance. It's usually accompanied by a lame, insincere apology, often blaming 'technical difficulties', 'administrative errors', or other unlikely and unbelievable explanations. The Train Operating Companies and their apologist poodle, The Rail

Delivery Group are masters at this waffle and subterfuge, and of course, now have serious competition from BA!

But something different happened with HomeServe. They acted quickly, responsibly and authentically, and I was fortunate enough to learn more about how they achieved this when I met Greg Reed, HomeServe Membership CEO and *Chief HomeServe Evangelist*, one of the key drivers on the road to recovery. While Greg, along with HomeServe UK CEO Martin Bennett, led the charge and created a culture of top down - bottom up innovation, they had the full support of colleagues throughout the organizations who saw this as a real opportunity to transform HomeServe and make it an organization they could all be proud of.

Individuals that have experienced traumatic events, whether self-inflicted addictions or circumstantial, and have survived, often seem to come through the other side the better for it and exercise tremendous determination to recover and be a better person. You need look no further than many of the injured service men and women, who have gone on to lead full and rewarding lives, despite their hardships. Achieving that as a company is not as easy. It takes true leadership from the top, commitment from the troops and an unwavering, uncompromising belief in doing the right thing. Which in a business sense, means doing the right thing **for the customer**, not just today, not just for a few, but forever and for the many.

This was going to take a whole new attitude, a whole new awareness of what *'customer'* really meant, and a commitment to continue to change the culture from sales-focused to customer-centric. Easy to say, but as many businesses have found out, much more difficult to achieve unless you have everyone on board and they believe and trust in the destination in equal measure.

A New Beginning – Customer First (yes really!)

In 2014, following the FCA fine, HomeServe needed to recover financially, organizationally and reputationally. To make this happen, Martin, Greg and the senior executive team developed a forward-looking strategy which they called *Effortless 2020*, and they set out their stall to be the UK's number one home assistance company.

It was clear that reducing customer effort and nurturing an innovation culture would be critical elements, as they required the full support and buy-in from the whole organization, especially the front line. One of the most important key initiatives, was the idea of *Customer First*. In HomeServe's universe 96% of the 2000+ jobs they complete in customers' homes each day are completed the same day and go off without any issues. When it is a straightforward claim within the policy then it is simple. What happens though when it isn't straight forward? What happens when the customer is not insured according to the terms, but the front line person wants to help them because they have been loyal or are vulnerable? How do you empower people to make that decision?

Greg Reed thought he had the answer and in some honest, soul searching sessions with his colleagues, he decided that they would just ask their people to send examples of customer issues they'd like help resolving, or processes that needed improving. A cross-functional team would review the requests first thing the following morning with remedial action agreed and implemented as quickly as possible. The new 'baby' was conceived now it was time to "Call the Midwife", and Gemma Hammond was ready and waiting to deliver!

Computer says No – People say Yes!

You'll remember that Gemma wanted to help Margaret MacDonald earlier in our story, but organizational indifference and an unhealthy desire for profit made that impossible. Now she could act. Now she could make a difference. Now she could show the compassion that came naturally to her. Gemma had compiled a list of all those vulnerable customers that had requested help and suggested this was a starting point for *Customer First*, they would contact them and get an update on their situation and where possible, and appropriate, provide a solution. Margaret McDonald was one of the first people that she called. After checking to make sure all was well, Gemma was able to assure her that she would never be left in the cold again, and that HomeServe would always be proactive in ensuring her needs would be met.

Since then Gemma has gone onto to be a champion of the *Customer First* program with almost over 125 referrals to the *Customer First* team and is an inspiration to her many front line colleagues who also make significant referrals.

Martin Bennett and the other execs have reinforced the *Customer First* message consistently over the past 18 months and it is now part of the fabric of the business. Over two thousand people have now made submissions to the program demonstrating what engaged and committed colleagues can do and allowing the front line people to really own and influence the customer experience.

Powered by People, fuelled by Compassion, Reassurance and Enthusiasm

Customer First has also played a key role in implementing many of the other elements of the 2020 strategy. The submissions were categorized as either 'Good Neighbour' or 'Business Improvement'. Based on that feedback, this guided the investment in process re-engineering and technology to reduce customer effort and make life easier for front line specialists and engineers to drive more value for customers. This also had a positive impact in reducing the cost base by eliminating unworkable policies, reducing waste and driving overall efficiencies.

None of this happened overnight and the big difference is that Home Serve has empowered their staff at all levels to do the right thing. This can only be done if you set up a democratic style of leadership where the 'People' play a key role. Having front line people identifying customer issues is just the start of the process.

But to really affect lasting change, and to make *Customer First* the real deal, consistent communication throughout the business, as well as strong community spirit, are basic tenets of the program. Consequently the *Customer First* team led by Sohib Hussain and Tony Bishop are in constant dialogue with everyone associated with any customer issue to make sure that nothing falls through the cracks, and in helping one customer they don't inadvertently disadvantage another. This takes understanding, creativity and trust on many levels, and there are healthy and visible supplies of the latter on display. A great example of this is the on-site shop. It has no staff and works on the honour system serving an unlimited supply of honest, caring and trusted people.

But you can't just say "We trust you" and then walk away. It's an ongoing and natural key cultural element that must be constantly fed and nurtured and then allowed to permeate the whole business. The resulting theme is *"Together we'll take care of it"*, which the whole business has literally signed up to and is a constant and daily reminder of this commitment. It's underpinned by *"Our People Promises"* and *"Our Customer Promises"*, which are also prominently displayed throughout the building and are the cornerstones of the culture of trust in each other and their shared responsibility towards all customers.

Put the right tools in the right hands and watch them go:

HomeServe also recognized that even with a healthy dose of good intentions, empowerment and enthusiasm, colleagues needed to be enabled by the right technology to allow them to really shine. Consequently there is an ongoing and carefully orchestrated program to roll-out solutions based on readily and easily accessible customer interaction data, that is personalized, relevant and immediately beneficial to the customer and colleagues. Customers reach out from many places, in different ways and usually without much warning. What they want more than anything is recognition of who they are, what their issues are and how quickly and smoothly it will be addressed and then, that the person they're speaking with has the full context in order to satisfy their interaction smoothly and completely. As part of a key transformation towards a more digital operation, HomeServe has also embraced social media and web-chat to make sure that they're available to speak to customers via their channel of choice, which in today's world is becoming increasingly important for all customers.

And it's not just improving technology for the sake of customers, which of course is critical to great customer service. HomeServe has also realized that agent engagement is vital to delivering an outstanding customer experience. Implementing a digital strategy requires cross-functional collaboration, and along with Greg Reed, HomeServe's CIO Lesley Ashman has been very prominent in engaging front line people in the process. That means listening to advisers, understanding their biggest frustrations, encouraging a generation of new ideas and removing potential barriers for customers.

Four key lessons from HomeServe:

The HomeServe journey should be required reading as part of any customer experience user manual, and there's a cornucopia of learning for any company striving for excellence in customer experience. However, if I had to distil it down to my top four lessons, they would be these.

1. Empower Employees

Make it personal and let them be themselves

Empower can be an overused word, and often there are large perceptual gaps between a company's ambitions and employee reality. But the concept is critical to success, and is about giving employees permission to engage with customers on an emotional and personal level. There should some guidelines and you don't want them giving away the store, but the customer service agent owns 'the moment', feels the pulse of the customer and has the greatest impact on the customer experience in the initial interactions. The best companies enhance their customer engagement by encouraging employees to build on their natural feelings, emotions and attitudes and do the right thing – for the customer.

2. Enable the Organization

Where agility, flexibility and adaptability trump dumb rules

Even if an employee is totally empowered, enablement means they have the right tools, accurate data, operational knowledge and organizational incentives to overcome procedural roadblocks and dumb company rules to really execute against your customer engagement strategy. It's about creating an environment in which employees are continuously provided with the right information, at the right time and the encouragement to take affirmative action, and not be constricted by policies and procedures that worked fine in the 1950s, but aren't fit for purpose now.

Customer inspired companies such as HomeServe, realize that customer service and the customer experience are not based on all customers being equal and eschew a 'one size fits all' strategy. They align their processes, empower their staff and have the enabling technology to make sure that each customer interaction is relevant, personalized and satisfying, for both customer and colleague.

3. Engage and Communicate with Customers

Right Message, Right Time, Right People, Right Result

In an increasingly commoditized world, organizations must focus on how they can differentiate themselves. This can be how they engage and connect with customers on an individual, personal basis and is often found to be the missing piece in the engagement puzzle.

HomeServe has discovered that having their web-chat team engage promptly with customers means they can identify those who are having an issue in real-time, and can conduct proactive support that greatly improves the transactional, touch point customer experience and contributes positively to the full customer journey. It also increases the chances of first time resolution and unnecessary repeat contacts, which plays a key role in keeping a handle on costs and when combined affords the best result and a great outcome for all stakeholders.

4. Embed a culture of excellence

Defined by the customer, refined by the people

Many companies talk nonchalantly about excellence as if it were something they could bestow on themselves. The best, and in fact the only, arbiters of excellence are customers. They will define what great service is and what satisfaction means to them, and will be the ongoing barometer of excellence in your business.

Creating an environment where listening, hearing, understanding and acting becomes second nature is critical to achieving consistently high levels of customer satisfaction. But that's only half the battle. To truly be best in class, and to develop and embed this culture of excellence, organizations must effectively leverage their talent, technology, and metrics to proactively anticipate and fulfil customer needs and expectations.

Employees who are trusted, treated well and empowered, have the tools and knowledge to succeed and the ability to use them wisely and are held accountable, but have authority, can really delight customers and make each experience, regardless of complexity, a memorable one that will have customers coming back for more.

In the end the key to this is consistency. Just having the playbook and the strategy is not enough; they've got to be used every day with every customer, across every channel and every interaction.

The Best News - The most improved company and even the bottom line comes out on top

Much of HomeServe's earlier struggles came as a result of a focus on profit rather than customers. So, it would be natural to expect that to regain customers and colleagues trust it would be necessary to make changes that could have an adverse effect on the bottom line. But as with many companies that take a more ethical and customer focused approach, they found out that by doing the right thing for the right reasons, but not forgetting to do things right, the money actually followed and financial performance improved. In the most recent reporting period ending March 31, 2017, customer numbers rose by 11%, revenue grew by 24% and profit by 20%.

However, it's not just profits that are up. An independent survey has shown that HomeServe, is delivering on its customer promises to provide effortless service, with the most improved customer satisfaction in the services industry since the Institute of customer service began measuring it.

They have also been named Best Home Emergency Cover Provider by Moneynet for the second year running, and Bloomberg has rated HomeServe as the Best Employer in Business Services in the UK, following an independent employee survey. This was confirmed by Glassdoor who named HomeServe as one of the top three best places to work in the UK.

The HomeServe Army – Guardians of Integrity and Ethical Behaviour

When sporting teams and company shares record improvement that belies their previous poor performance, often as a result of a new manager, the term 'dead cat bounce' is often used to describe this phenomenon. Feline elasticity rarely lasts long and is not really strategically viable over the long term, but with HomeServe it's a very different type of bounce. While the initial charge was led by a few inspired and committed souls, the army was quickly mobilized and the job of sustaining and keeping alive the innovation culture is now in many strong hands, and Is filled with the energy and commitment that comes from 3,142 guardians of integrity and ethical behaviour. They won't let this one get away.

In the end, what I discovered at HomeServe, is that they've based their culture of excellence on a strong set of core values, and a code of behaviour that, as I noted earlier, is reflected frequently and visually throughout the HomeServe offices as their documented commitments to customers and each other. Neither is an empty promise, nor a hastily devised marketing slogan and are in fact both living, breathing statements of intent that represent the true beating heart of the business. This is not mandated solely from above, but is based on shared beliefs, values, and practices. The company understand that one of the key outputs from increased employee engagement is, where all of the employees have a strong voice that they are not afraid to exercise and are directly responsible for developing the fundamentals on which their service culture is built, and that will keep it alive.

It's people like Gemma Hammond, Sohib Hussain, Tony Bishop, Greg Reed, and Martin Bennett who, combined with the other resolute guardians of the future, have turned a small drop of compassion into a flood of goodwill, and burst open the doors to showcase a great business!

Autoglass® has a clear vision for a great customer experience

It was a dark and stormy night. The woman, stranded by the side of a motorway on the rawest of December days, shivered and peered anxiously into her rear view mirror hoping to see the reassuring lights of the breakdown service van that was coming to change her tyre. "Two hours" they said, and, as her mobile phone was running desperately low on power, she couldn't even risk calling home in case the RAC couldn't find her, and she needed to call again.

Then a brightly lit vehicle pulled up and her spirits immediately lifted; she thought "Thank God, they're early." But it wasn't the RAC, it was even better than that. It was Gavin from Autoglass® – well, it wasn't actually Gavin, but someone just as good. But wait a minute Autoglass® don't fix tyres do they? The clue would seem to be in the name. No, but what they do very well is empathy and compassion. They are frequent motorway 'Heroes', who stop to help motorists, especially in times of obvious dire need.

Bill Kalyan, former Head of Sales and Service Centre at the Autoglass® head-quarters in Bedford, shared this great customer story on a recent visit. This is one of many similar communications from customers who have experienced a level of care rarely seen in any business in the UK. I was there to learn why Autoglass® has become a household name. Calling Autoglass® is a distress purchase, and as Bill said, "I'm sure none of you have said to your partner; 'hey, why don't we go out and look at new windscreens today'."

Despite this, Autoglass® has generated a significant following on Facebook and Twitter, showing how important it is to create a strong presence and positive sentiment out in social media land, even if there isn't an immediate need for your product.

But this isn't really just about social media, (though more on how Bill and his team have driven the digital and mobile revolution at Autoglass® later on). This is how an organization that started in Bedford in 1972, grew to be a leading consumer automotive service brand, providing vehicle glass repairs and replacements to over 1 million motorists every year. Autoglass® has over 100 branches nationwide and 1,200 mobile technicians serving customers 24 hours a day, seven days a week, 365 days a year. That's the history lesson, but it really doesn't tell the whole story.

Autoglass® is primarily a service provider to the insurance industry, but also serves motorists directly. Being able to empathetically and promptly deal with the types of difficulties that we find ourselves in when a windscreen goes pop is critical to their success. This positivity, and the customer experience that it delivers, finds its source in the mantra that wafts through the business like a refreshing summer breeze; *"A natural willingness to make a difference for our customers"*. This is no empty promise or glib marketing slogan. It is based on a deeply shared, mutually developed and socialized value system that is aligned to the overall business culture. This reflects the commitment of both employees and management, and is based on fundamental and proven principles.

The four fundamental principles that drive customer experience

These four principles; Culture, Commitment, Community and Communication, are the lifeblood of a truly customer centric organization. They are the foundation on which Bill and his team have built their customer experience strategy, and in a broader context govern human effectiveness and conscious thought. They have been vital and visibly active components in establishing a foundation for the processes, tools, technologies and practices that have transformed Autoglass® by engaging the whole company and bringing the operational side of their customer experience strategy to life.

Culture drives the business forward

The culture of excellence that has grown up over the last few years at Autoglass® has given the customer service centre the guidance, tools and authority to make timely decisions. They are clearly proud of what they do and the role they play in rescuing customers in need. Most are smartly attired in, and are empowered by, an Autoglass® 'uniform' , and it certainly feels as if this contributes to the high quality and friendly, confident approach to customers shown by the contact centre, branch and mobile technician workforce. It's clear that Autoglass® has recognized that people really do make a difference, especially when given the right level of training, trust and authority to make decisions, solve problems and keep customers informed.

Doing business with Autoglass® is easy

A lot has been written about the importance of making life easy for customers and reducing effort. Nowhere is this more important than when you're staring at a pile of broken glass and getting a face full of fresh air. Paradoxically, as many businesses have found out, making it easy and delighting customers aren't mutually exclusive and take a lot of hard work. Regardless of whether you measure delight, effort or ease of doing business, at some point you will need to drill down into the root causes of customer perceptions: what specific technologies, business processes and/or employee behaviours made doing business with the company easy or difficult? This is where Bill and his team focused their energies, and the customer feedback reflects this. Autoglass® is rated as one of the top customer service providers in the UK, as measured by a Net Promoter Score (NPS), which has consistently rated over 75% over the last three years, compared to many other businesses that typically 'achieve' scores in the lower category.

Technology supports the vision

Technology clearly plays a key role in making this happen. Autoglass® has made sure that they have aligned their ambition with the corresponding technology to meet evolving customer demands and expectations, while at the same time ensuring that it provides the capability for smooth and speedy processes for the customer service teams. This is particularly true of the evolution of the digital and mobile channels that are playing an increasingly important role at Autoglass®. Consequently, as with any truly innovative organization that really understands the Omni-channel world, they have invested heavily to ensure that their digital and mobile strategy, and the underlying technology, reflects the customer choice of channels, is seamless integrated and device agnostic.

The Customer Relationship Management (CRM) system is a rich and growing source of data that is tightly integrated with insurance company systems. This quickly allows the advisors to bring up the relevant information on the customer, the vehicle and the associated insurance details. This means that rather than navigating sluggishly through myriad screens, the Autoglass® advisor typically has all of the relevant information on a single screen, and can quickly confidently and professionally complete the transaction regardless of the channel.

Digital and Mobile strategy keeps pace with a changing world

In the early days much of the business was done via the local service centres, especially in the dark days before mobile phones came along to 'liberate' us all. Currently, 95% of the initial interactions are handled online or through the contact centre by phone, or via webchat Autoglass® ambition is to have 75% of interactions electronic by 2018, and they are on track to meet this objective. The website is impressive and functionally friendly, and clearly shows the phone number, the call-back option, and an on-line booking capability on every page. Navigation is simple and logical, information is easy to find, with key items such as pricing and replacement logistics being transparent and complete.

Autoglass® also recognized that social media was becoming more important to their customers, and in 2011 became the first UK service company to launch an integrated Facebook App for bookings, with the added bonus of being able to engage customers in a broader brand feedback discussion. As a result of their very successful TV ads featuring Gavin, the technician, Facebook groups sprang up with thousands of people talking about him and his role in the company. This showed that despite the distress nature of the purchase, people were legitimately interested in interacting with the company, perhaps for a little in fun at first, but also because for many having a windscreen problem wasn't an everyday occurrence. It gave Autoglass® an opportunity to play a market leading role, providing a genuinely valuable and timely service.

Once you put yourself out there, it's even more important that you can respond quickly and authoritatively to both positive and negative posts. Autoglass® has had their share of the latter, and clearly being able to deal with these quickly, while addressing the core problem, is of vital importance. Bill introduced me to Emma and Mike who are up in the 'Twitter sphere' and he was clearly proud of the role they play in responding promptly to any Facebook or Twitter posts. It's not a perfect world, and even Autoglass® sometimes make a mistake, but when they do, and especially if the customer lets the world know via social media, Emma and Mike are quick to step in and calm the situation down. What's great about it is that they are located with the rest of their colleagues in the service centre, have access to all customer data, and take total responsibility for any problem that comes their way and then see it through to a usually happy ending.

It wasn't always like this though. Bill told me that when he first started, 26 years ago (Alex Ferguson was also job hunting then, but had to settle for Man U!) and for many years after, the contact centre was a small, dark room where the employees were kept under lock and key for 8 hours, and only allowed out for brief comfort breaks and the occasional thimble full of water. Perhaps I overstate, but you get my drift and, as with many businesses, they were seen as a disconnected cost centre and certainly not integrated into the rest of the business, either culturally, physically or technologically.

Consequently, as a result of the trust instilled in them and the encouragement, support and commitment from Bill and the rest of the management team - along with technology that helps, not hinders - the contact centre team knows that as far as the customer is concerned, they are the company, and respond enthusiastically and positively to each new challenge.

There are many reasons for the success of Autoglass®, but I couldn't help but feel while sitting in the contact centre and talking with the team, a highly charged flow of supportive energy that pulsates through the business.

While Autoglass® still has some work to do to consistently deliver a great customer experience; they can see the road ahead, have great faith in their travelling companions and a clear vision of where they're going and how to get there.

I'd certainly put my chips on them and all the team; loading up the van, driving more customer advocacy and delivering the goods.

Metro Bank – A delightful and daringly different banking experience

I was recently very honored to get a new and titled follower, along with a retweet on Twitter. In fact, this follower has two titles, which, considering he's a dog and is associated with a bank is even more impressive. Of course, recent history has shown us that titled bankers, or former titled bankers, aren't necessarily guarantees of success or wellbeing – unless it's their own.

I speak of course about Sir Duffield II, Chief Canine Officer at Metro Bank, who, along with the rest of those wild and crazy guys and girls at Metro, the UK's first new High Street bank in over 100 years, are part of a game changing revolution in financial services in the UK. You've had enough of bankers that are wild and crazy? Especially with your money. Well, I didn't mean Fred the Shred, or the Diamond Geezer. I mean people that are wild and crazy, along with being passionate and committed about delivering a banking experience, and making a personal connection that is truly unique and different – not only from other banks, but from most other businesses.

Time for a change – A bank you can love

Now we all know that banking has been in need of a serious shake-up for a long time. Many traditional banks are trying to walk the talk with ads that abound with "Customers are at the heart of our business" or "we're always there for you" etc., but their history of appalling service, disdain for their customers and unbridled greed can't be quickly erased, or forgotten with hastily crafted mission statements, or empty marketing slogans.

So what's different about Metro Bank?

- No stupid bank rules
- Unlimited dog biscuits (for your canine friend of course)
- Free Pens – a truly Unchained Melody
- Free cash counting machines
- Smiling, friendly, welcoming people who love what they do – and it shows
- Delivering a great retail experience

You may think that these are just headline makers, or that I'm also a little crazy for supporting an organization that has a dog in a key position and a warehouse full of dog biscuits. But you'd be barking up the wrong tree. These are key foundations of Metro Bank's core principles and have made their motto "Love your Bank at Last", a genuine and visible symbol of a business whose culture matches their model.

They recognize that by focusing on service and convenience, creating a pleasant and welcoming environment, staffed by people who have fun and really care, they are truly able to develop an emotional bond that creates 'fans', not customers. As a result, it's no surprise that people who embrace their model and become part of a community, are more than willing to become brand advocates and share their great experiences with friends to generate referrals that are the life blood of any successful business. How many of us are truly 'proud' of our association with our current bank and will tell others? That's what I thought.

Making it happen – The devil's in the detail

Metro Bank didn't just figure this out and hope for the best. Metro Bank founder, Vernon Hill, had already proven the model in the US when he founded Commerce Bank in 1973, and grew it from a single location to 440 stores across six States. The decision to operate as a retail business, not a bank, and to focus on the detail and the execution at the point of customer contact, Is one of the key competitive differentiators from traditional banking operations.

As with any successful retail operation, Metro Bank has made a huge investment in facilities, training and people. Walking into one of their colorful, bright and refreshingly welcoming stores, you're immediately struck by the fact that the staff are actually glad to see you. Clearly, there isn't an additional fee for smiling, greeting you warmly and helping you feed the Magic Money counting machine. That alone is worth the trip. But being human, having fun (and not being a bunch of bankers), or taking themselves too seriously, doesn't detract from the staff's total commitment and passion, and the surprise and delight that dealing with caring, sharing people will bring.

Metro Bank has made a serious and on-going investment into attracting, educating and retaining the best people. Their mantra "Hire for attitude, Train for skill" continues to pay handsome dividends to customers and fellow staff members alike, and is one of the most important reasons for Metro Bank's success. As with other successful organizations, it's clear that both the employee experience and a great customer experience are inextricably linked, and I've been fortunate to hear first-hand how some of their people feel about being part of this great journey.

Here are some of their thoughts:

"I said in my very first interview that I hope to spend the rest of my career at Metro Bank and I stand by that to this day. I work with the most amazing people and as part of a growing, exciting company the sky really is the limit."

"Working in the contact centre has been a real journey for me. I love being able to offer my colleagues and our customers the support and guidance that they need, and constantly instill our culture as we grow."

"Metro Bank is the career I've always wanted, and the opportunities for growth and personal development are endless."

Everyone isn't a perfect fit to be on the Metro Bank team, and their selection criteria, while stringent, ensures that the fit is right for both the employee and Metro Bank. Consequently the ones that make the grade, understand that by delivering superior service and building long term relationships, both they and the customers will be better off for the experience.

A bank that leads from the heart and feeds the soul

There's no question that Metro Bank has set out to make an emotional and heartfelt assault on the UK financial services industry, and by doing so, are changing people's feelings and their expectations about 'banks' forever. I call this banking for the soul, because it nourishes and feeds our fundamental needs as human beings, tops up our emotional bank account and pays life changing interest on a regular basis. For Metro Bank fans and employees alike, it has long term, sustainable and desirable benefits beyond a simple deposit and a regular pay cheque.

The beating heart of any organization is fueled by the flow of spirit, emotion and energy that the employees pump out every day. But, for this to happen, there must be a healthy supply of truly engaged and inspired people for whom the organization has magnetic appeal and forges an almost unbreakable bond. Where an environment of innovation and ambition is generated by giving employees more than the boon of occupation, this creates a spirit of mutual respect and true sharing and ownership in the business that is a powerful and rewarding experience for all. This is why Metro Bank is truly different, and why it means so much more than just a 'bank' for their fans, their people, and of course, Spot and Fido.

28814696R00103

Printed in Great Britain
by Amazon